How to Use
Discussion
in the
Classroom
The Complete Guide

Mike Gershon

1400 Centrepark Blvd., Ste 1000
West Palm Beach, FL 33401
717.845.6300
email: pub@learningsciences.com
learningsciences.com

Printed in the United States of America

22   21   20   19   18   1   2   3   4   5

Names: Gershon, Mike, author.

Title: How to use discussion in the classroom : the complete guide / Mike Gershon.

Description: West Palm Beach, FL : Learning Sciences, 2018. | Series: Great teaching made easy. | Previously released in the UK in 2013 by Mike Gershon.

Identifiers: LCCN 2018945746 | ISBN 978-1-943920-47-1 (pbk.) | ISBN 978-1-943920-48-8 (ebook)

Subjects: LCSH: Discussion--Study and teaching. | Student growth (Academic achievement) | Education--Aims and objectives. | Learning, Psychology of. | Effective teaching. | BISAC: EDUCATION / Professional Development. | EDUCATION / Teaching Methods & Materials / General. | EDUCATION / Aims & Objectives.

Classification: LCC LB1060 .G47 2018 (print) | LCC LB1060 (ebook) | DDC 370.15--dc23.

Series Introduction

The 'How to…' series developed out of Mike Gershon's desire to share great classroom practice with teachers around the world. He wanted to put together a collection of books which would help professionals no matter what age group or subject they were teaching.

Each volume focuses on a different element of classroom practice and each is overflowing with brilliant, practical strategies, techniques and activities – all of which are clearly explained and ready-to-use. In most cases, the ideas can be applied immediately, helping teachers not only to teach better but to save time as well.

All of the books have been designed to help teachers. Each one goes out of its way to make educators' lives easier and their lessons even more engaging, inspiring and successful than they already are.

In addition, the whole series is written from the perspective of a working teacher. It takes account of the realities of the classroom, blending theoretical insight with a relentlessly practical focus.

The 'How to…' series is great teaching made easy.

Author Introduction

Mike Gershon is a teacher, trainer and writer. He is the author of over forty books on teaching, learning and education, including a number of bestsellers, as well as the co-author of four others. Mike's online resources have been viewed and downloaded more than 3.5 million times by teachers in over 180 countries and territories. He writes for the *Times Educational Supplement* and has created over eighty guides to different areas of teaching and learning as well as two online courses covering outstanding teaching and growth mindsets. Find out more, get in touch and download free resources at www.mikegershon.com or www.learning sciences.com/mikegershon.

Acknowledgments

First and foremost I must thank Jeremy Hayward, who taught me to teach. He has been a major influence and he is, without doubt, the best teacher I know. Thanks also to the many great teachers I have had over the years, specifically Judith Schofield, Richard Murgatroyd, Simon Mason, Cath Nealon, Andrew Gilliland, Graham Ferguson, and Simon Ditchfield. I must also thank all the wonderful teachers I have worked with and learnt from at Central Foundation Girls' School, Nower Hill High School, Pimlico Academy and King Edward VI School, Bury St Edmunds. Special mention must go to the Social Sciences team at Pimlico, to Jon Mason and to James Wright. Of course, I cannot fail to thank all the fantastic students I have had the pleasure of teaching – particularly all the members of HC and HD at Pimlico. In addition, I am greatly indebted to the people I trained with at the IOE and, in particular, to Erin, Liam, Anna and Rahwa. Finally, thanks to my mum for her unfailing support over the years and her wonderful example.

I have picked up many of the activities, strategies and techniques in this book from the countless wonderful people I have worked with; however, any errors or omissions remain my own.

Table of Contents

CHAPTER ONE

Introduction

Welcome to *How to Use Discussion in the Classroom: The Complete Guide*. Contained within is a wealth of practical ideas which teachers can pick up and begin using immediately, no matter what age group they teach, or what area of the curriculum they specialise in.

This is a book which will help you to improve your own classroom practice, as well as the learning experience of your students.

Everything has been written with the busy teacher in mind. The strategies, techniques and activities which follow are all ready-to-use and take account of the practicalities of day-to-day teaching.

This is a book which will help you to be a brilliant teacher.

It is a book which will help you to raise achievement.

It is a book that will help you to make your classroom an engaging, motivational environment in which learning is at the top of everyone's agenda.

If you want to dive straight in, head to chapter 2: Strategies and Techniques. The practical material starts there. It continues in chapter 3: Activities.

Chapter 2 explains and exemplifies twenty strategies and techniques which can be used to facilitate high-quality discussion. It also outlines extensions and developments for each of these.

Chapter 3 does exactly the same except with twenty classroom activities. Each one of these is generic and simply requires the teacher to insert whatever subject-specific content they want students to think about and talk about.

Chapter 4 does the same but with a further twenty activities. I have split the chapters in order to make navigation easier. A brief conclusion draws the book to a close.

If you want to explore discussion before looking at how to use it, keep reading this introduction. Three aspects are briefly outlined. They are:

- The relative strengths and weaknesses of the three generic discussion-types: paired discussion, group discussion and whole-class discussion.
- The relationships between speaking, writing, thinking and knowledge.
- The ideas of three key theorists – John Dewey, Neil Mercer and Lev Vygotsky – which inform many of the ideas in this book.

I have not chosen to include a specific section in which the case is made for discussion as a teaching method. This is because the argument is advanced by the book as a whole and because I believe such a section would detract from the central focus: practical strategies ready to be used by teachers in their classrooms, no matter what it is they are teaching.

Of course, it is up to you how you use the book. My own suggestion would be to see it as a compendium of ideas which can be taken on and embedded in your own pedagogy or used to plan engaging, inspiring and enjoyable lessons. However you choose to use it, I am sure that it will bring significant benefits to your professional practice and to the learning experience of your students.

Paired, Group and Whole-Class Discussion

In the activities section of this book you can find many examples of how to structure discussion. Paired, group and whole-class discussion can also be generic, though. Knowing when to opt for one method in favour of another is a skill which teachers develop over time. What follows is broad guidance that should be taken in conjunction with the understanding that comes (or will come, depending what stage of your career you are at) with experience.

Paired discussion is a valuable aid to whole-class teaching. It can be used with ease throughout a lesson. The only requirement is that pupils can find a partner quickly and that disruption is kept to a minimum. This usually means students working with the person who is sat next to them; it may sometimes involve one or more students moving or turning around.

The great benefit of using paired discussion is that the teacher rarely has to create any resources or establish a detailed structure. They can simply indicate a question, statement or topic which is to be talked about before requesting that students discuss it with their partner. Here is an example:

Teacher: OK, before we start to investigate the functions of the digestive system, turn to your partner and discuss what you think the functions might be.

Such an instruction is likely to come near the start of the lesson. A further example:

Teacher: In a moment we will review what we have learnt this lesson. First, I would like you to spend five minutes discussing your work with your partner. Identify what you think you have done well and what could be improved. Find evidence to support what you say.

This instruction would come near the end of a lesson. It contains more detail than the first one and, as a result, will lead to a more structured discussion; there is a precise purpose, which is to underpin what students do. This differs from the first case, in which the teacher's intention was to elicit students' prior knowledge.

Paired discussion is of benefit to pupils as well as being useful for teachers. This book makes clear what can be achieved through a pedagogy which includes discussion. By giving students the opportunity to discuss in pairs, the teacher is allowing the greatest number of pupils the chance to share their thoughts and to explore their understanding.

Speaking and listening are the rudiments of discussion. Because only one person is allowed to speak at a time, all forms of discussion will see the majority of students listening. Paired discussion, in which every 'group' consists of only two members, allows all members of a class the greatest opportunity to speak. Students are competing for air-time with only one other person and a discussion will not ensue unless both parties accept that they will have to make a contribution. Paired discussion is thus a powerful tool for ensuring all students in a class are able to participate fully in debate.

The final thing to note before we move on is that paired discussion tends to work well as a starting point for other activities or tasks. The two examples given above both demonstrate this. Of course, paired discussion can stand alone – just as it can be highly structured or supplemented by extra resources – but, generally, it will work in concert with another activity or as part of a tapestry of tasks or processes. It is a technique as much as an independent entity; one which the teacher can use to develop thinking, elicit knowledge or lead into other pieces of work.

In contrast to paired discussion, group discussion usually requires more structure and greater planning. There is one important reason for this.

When students are grouped in threes, fours or fives (the traditional numbers found in group activities) there is the potential for some pupils to disengage, leaving it to others to do the work. When challenged on this, many will point to the fact that other members of the group are taking part in discussion as a justification for their own behaviour. The rationale is that as long as the work is being done then everything is OK.

For us as teachers this is obviously not the case. Our aim is to have all members of the class engaged in whatever work has been set so that they are all learning. For the teacher, the work is not instrumental. It is an end in itself. As such, it is important to forestall the unwanted behaviour to which group discussion may give rise. This can be done through careful planning which includes things such as:

- Allocating roles
- Providing a structure which encompasses all participants
- Separating the group discussion into mini-discussions which are subsequently shared
- Thinking carefully about which students are grouped together
- Providing discussion topics which are accessible to all

Despite requiring extra prior input from the teacher, group discussion in action tends to see students given greater freedom and independence. For the method to be worthwhile, the teacher needs to step back. Having provided a structure for the discussion, they must leave pupils to their own devices (while maintaining a watchful eye, of course).

In group discussion, there is a greater ceding of control by the teacher than is the case in either paired or whole-class discussion. Two points arise from this. First, the teacher must be *prepared* to cede control. Group discussion will be severely impeded if the teacher keeps intervening, for example, by continually drawing the class's attention in order to make teaching points. The main purpose of group discussion, it may be argued, is for students to lead their own learning through a framework set out by the teacher.

Second, there may be some classes where the behaviour issues which result from the ceding of control outweigh any benefits. In these cases there are two options open to the teacher:

1. Attempt to train the class over a period of time so that they are capable of discussing successfully in groups. This will involve the gradual introduction of group elements to discussion tasks and the establishing of ground rules in paired and whole-class discussion which can be transferred to group discussion.
2. Do not do group discussion with the class. This is not the end of the world; you can still use paired and whole-class discussion as well as a range of other activities. It is better to acknowledge that a certain class struggles with an activity type than to continue using it despite the problems which it throws up.

Drawing the previous few points together, we can note that group discussion carries higher risks than paired and whole-class discussion, but that it also has higher pay-offs as well. A really successful group discussion – in which three, four or five students are exploring ideas, challenging one another and working in unison to construct knowledge and develop understanding – is an incredibly rich learning experience. That is why, despite the potential difficulties which come with the approach, it is worth pursuing.

We turn finally to whole-class discussion. This usually sees the teacher standing at the front of the room with the whole class sat before them (an alternative approach sees teacher and students sat together in a large circle).

It is a method which allows the teacher to retain the maximum level of control over their pupils. They are the focal point for the class and in a position to direct proceedings. This can include a stipulation that all comments must pass through the teacher (in as much as they will choose who is to speak).

The approach is good for establishing wider ground rules which subsequently permeate all other types of discussion. These usually include the following guiding principles: only one person is to speak at any one time, and all contributions and contributors are to be treated with respect. The teacher's role as head of the discussion (judge, facilitator, director) allows them to deal with rule breaches and to praise students for doing the right thing.

One of the biggest benefits of whole-class discussion is that it has the greatest possible number of contributors. This means there is the potential for students to hear a diversity of opinions which may not be accessible in paired or group discussion. Exposure to a wide range of ideas is likely to lead to developments in understanding (not least by greying that which might previously have been viewed as black and white). It is also likely to encourage creative thinking. Bringing disparate perspectives together may give rise to original thoughts. This is because a larger number of contributions will mean a larger number of potential contribution-combinations. Innovative or unusual suggestions often come forth due to the sheer increase in numbers.

The last point to note concerning whole-class discussion is that it has greater theatricality than paired or group discussion. The teacher, at the front of the class, is in a position to embellish and dramatize contributions which students make (or which they themselves provide). This presents the opportunity to engage and motivate pupils. The teacher can draw them into the discussion through the use of rhetorical devices, acting and oratory. What is more, students can take advantage of this, if they wish, by using such techniques themselves, from wherever they are sitting or standing (though this is reliant to some extent on other pupils turning to look at them while they are speaking. The teacher may make this behaviour a rule and enforce it on the basis that it shows respect for the speaker and demonstrates active listening).

Speaking, Thinking, Writing and Knowledge

The infant child does not possess the power to articulate that which occurs inside of itself. One of the most difficult tasks parents first encounter is trying to establish what it is their baby wants when it exhibits distress, most often in the form of crying. They wish to ascertain this knowledge so that they can alter the situation; the desire to nurture a child physically and emotionally, to tend to its needs, is the overriding drive in nearly all parents.

On a brute rendering we may think of an infant's distress as their signal that all is not well. But what is it that is not well? It can only be something internal (such as the feeling of hunger) or external (such as loud noises heard through an open window). Yet, even in a case where the child's distress is caused by external stimuli, the experience of distress is still an internal one.

Let us imagine, for example, that a window has been left open to allow some fresh air into the house. After a time, the infant who is in the adjoining room begins to feel a draft. This makes them uncomfortable. They react to this discomfort by beginning to cry. Despite the fact, however, that this has been caused by an external stimulus (the cold air), the experience of the stimulus is still internal to the child. If the child's mother entered the room and happened, for some reason, to be insensitive to temperature, she would be hard pressed to identify the cause of the child's distress without undertaking a course of trial and error or a detailed examination of all the potential variables which could be affecting her son or daughter.

It is likely that the mother's presence, her picking up and holding of the baby, her talking and tending, would be sufficiently soothing to dispel the discomfort or anxiety which has occurred. It may be that through some method or other she could come to a conclusion about the role of the open window in causing her child's discomfort. What could certainly not happen, though, is any articulation by the baby of why it felt in distress.

Fast forward fifty years; she (let us say the baby was a girl by the name of Emily) who was once an infant is now a woman, and a poet to boot. Her latest collection includes a sonnet entitled 'Low Tide on Sandsend Beach'. In one particular couplet she evokes the experience of cold sea air running across naked arms, imbuing this with a sense and symbolism which it will take many readings to unravel. In an interview about her new book she explains how this particular part of the poem found its genesis in a brief conversation she had with a friend while visiting the Yorkshire Coast.

That which is internal to us – thoughts, sensations, feelings and emotions – can be made plain through language. Speech comes first. It is the precursor to writing. It is the means by which we communicate that which is inside us, and that which we experience, to others. The greater command one has over the spoken word, the more accurately one is able to give voice to one's own thoughts.

Just as language – speech – articulates thoughts, so too does it come to order and inform them. Think, for example, of the differing explanations a child and an adult might be able to provide of an event they both experience. The latter is a more knowledgeable and a more skilful user of language. This means that even before they share the same experience as the child, they will be primed to interpret it through a different (more developed) framework.

Using discussion in the classroom is important as it provides students with the opportunity to enhance their own frameworks of interpretation as well as their own skills in articulating that which they think, feel, sense or experience. This in turn has a knock-on effect on a student's ability to write.

The benefits of using discussion to precede writing are outlined elsewhere in this book. The central tenet is that the process of speaking about a subject allows one to manipulate one's thoughts about that subject. This means that writing about it is made easier; much of the hard work has already been done. Such work includes analysis, synthesis and evaluation of that which one thinks and knows about the topic in question. The ephemeral, instantly editable, unmediated nature of speech means that one can do things with it quickly and simply. Even the most skilled of writers will struggle to match this immediacy and easiness when manipulating the written word.

Let us consider an example through which we can demonstrate the benefits to be had from talking before writing.

Students are given the task of producing an essay which deals with the question of whether or not Queen Victoria was a good monarch. They are asked to discuss their ideas and to develop an essay plan. The following series of events might reasonably be expected to occur:

- Students discuss the question. They consider what the question means and how one might go about answering it. They also analyse some of the key words (in this case, the word 'good' is most at issue).
- Students discuss in further detail how to answer the question. They exchange ideas and then develop a single one in concert. They sketch a plan and then identify what one should write about and why.
- Students discuss the essay plan. They try to assess what exactly it is that the teacher wants. They exchange ideas about how best to write a plan. They then decide to write a plan together, using speech to develop their ideas.

By this point, students will each have an essay plan which they can use to structure their written work. The process of discussion will have led them to engage in a variety of tasks which could have been missed, made more difficult or taken far longer if no talking had been allowed.

What is more, if Student A and Student B engaged in discussion, it is highly likely that one or both will have said things of which the other simply hadn't thought (and, perhaps, never would have done). For example, Student A may have suggested that 'good' should be taken as referring to the things which Victoria did while Queen. Student B may have then interjected, pointing out that some of the things she did were viewed as good by some people and as bad by others.

The two main benefits which teachers and students can extract from the relationship between speech and writing are:

1. The improvements in thinking which are likely to result from hearing different people's ideas about a topic.
2. The speed and simplicity with which one can carry out intellectual work on a topic by talking about it (whether this is to precede writing or not).

Tied up with the first of these points is the issue of constructing knowledge. When a pair, group or whole class of students sit down together and discuss a topic, they are engaged in a process of knowledge creation. It is not so much that they are conjuring something from nothing, rather that they are building something from a series of smaller, pre-existing parts, the sum of which will be greater than the constituents. An example will be most helpful here:

Student A: In my opinion, Victoria was a good monarch because, for most of her reign, she was well-liked by the majority of her subjects.

Student B: I don't agree. Being liked does not necessarily mean she was good – people might have liked the image of her they had in their heads, rather than anything tangible or real. Also, by the nineteenth century it was politicians who ruled the country. Victoria didn't have any real power and so could not do much anyway. That means it is pointless assessing whether she was good or not.

Student A: Well, that's a fair point; politicians did rule the country and power had moved from the monarchy to parliament. Perhaps we should assess whether Victoria was a good monarch in the context of this arrangement. What did she do and what effects did it have? For example, being liked by the people may have helped to sustain the idea of the monarchy in its new, less powerful role. In that sense she was a good monarch – good for the future generations of the Royal Family.

We have a classic dialectic. Student A puts forward a thesis which Student B rebuts through an antithesis before Student A combines these ideas to form a synthesis. The final comment from Student A has its roots in the first two comments, but it is also qualitatively different. Something new has been constructed which would have been difficult for either student to access on their own.

The argument is that discussion allows the construction of knowledge and that because of this it is a good thing, benefitting students and helping them to learn.

Let us give another, more prosaic, example to reinforce the point:

Doctor: Good morning Mr Smith, what can I do for you today?

Mr Smith: Good morning doctor. Well I've not been feeling too good lately, so I thought I had better come and see you.

Doctor: What's been the matter?

Mr Smith: Well it's my foot you see. It hurts every time I put pressure on it. Like when I'm climbing the stairs, for example.

Doctor: I see. Tell me, Mr Smith, have you done anything which might have injured your foot in the past few weeks?

From here, the conversation would continue. There would also be a physical examination by the doctor. Matters would conclude with a diagnosis or a call for further investigation.

If Mr Smith had not spoken to the doctor, he would not have been able to convey that which was internal to him – the pain in his foot. If the doctor had not asked a series of questions, her understanding of Mr Smith's position would have been severely limited.

By the end of the discussion, the doctor will have provided Mr Smith with a diagnosis or will have explained to him the need for further investigation. Either scenario is an example of new knowledge. In the matter of diagnosis, the doctor is applying her existing knowledge and experience of medicine to the individual case of Mr Smith. In the matter of further investigation, the doctor is indicating that her knowledge does not allow her to accurately diagnose the situation and that something more will be required.

In both situations, the doctor and Mr Smith would have learnt something, with Mr Smith's learning being relatively greater and more valuable. The result, whichever it was, would have been a direct consequence of the separate contributions to the discussion made by each participant. If Mr Smith had not turned up, then the doctor, despite all her knowledge and skill, would not have been in a position to construct a diagnosis or to call for further tests. If the doctor had not turned up, Mr Smith would have been none the wiser about the state of his foot.

Discussion allows those taking part to construct new knowledge. Participants make contributions. These are predicated on their existing knowledge and understanding. The act of discussing involves thinking. Therefore, understanding is being developed. What is more, the combination of different ideas gives rise to the possibility of synthesis. Even if this is not achieved by the individuals engaged in a discussion, it is likely that everybody will leave with a broader set of ideas than they possessed at the start.

The two ways in which discussion helps to construct new knowledge are:

1. Thesis -> Antitheses -> Synthesis
2. Individual arrives at discussion with a frame of reference -> Individual leaves discussion with a larger frame of reference

Three Theorists – John Dewey

We will now look briefly at three influential theorists whose ideas concerning discussion inform the ideas presented in this book. First is John Dewey.

One of the central tenets of Dewey's philosophy was that education should be intimately bound up with democracy. It is not sufficient to learn by rote a set of facts about the world, or to leave school in possession of only that knowledge which is about the subjects one has studied. Rather, one should also come to understand what it means to be a part of society; one should learn how to live. Discussion is an important part of this.

Much of life involves talking about ideas or experiences and the attempt, through speech, to better understand something or to reach some kind of conclusion (perhaps linked to a subsequent action). Myriad examples make this point. We could call on instances from home life (How should we bring up our child? What is the best way to extend the house?), from work (What do you feel is the best way to secure this account? Where do people think we should go from here?), and even from the time we spend at leisure (How can Arsenal win the league next year? What do you think the ending of that drama serial meant?). It is because of this fact that we do well to use discussion in the classroom. We are preparing students for life by giving them present experience of a central tenet of our society.

Further, if we turn to the notion of democracy, we see that the very essence of such a political system is (or ought to be) discussion. In an autocracy, the word of the leader is final. What they say is an order to be obeyed. In a democracy, those who are in a position to wield power, or who wish to reach such a position, must persuade others that what they propose to do is something that ought to be done. The public and civic spheres provide spaces in which all parties can voice their opinions and put forward their arguments. Freedom of speech is protected so as to ensure that all ideas can be heard and that society is kept open for the benefit of everybody. As a result, using discussion in the classroom is akin to teaching for democracy; it fosters a democratic spirit in young people by letting them experience the ways of acting we seek to promote and sustain in society at large.

Three Theorists – Neil Mercer

Neil Mercer is, at the time of writing, Professor of Education at the University of Cambridge. A key aspect of his research into teaching and learning concerns the use of talk in the classroom. He has identified three different types which tend to form the basis of discussions:

- Disputational talk, in which claims and counter-claims are made. Two examples would be Prime Minister's Questions and the oral arguments presented by barristers in an appeal court. In each case, the talk in which participants are engaged is competitive and there is an expectation that, at the conclusion of the debate, there will be a winner. In the latter example this is a necessary part of the process; court cases must lead to a ruling one way or another. In the former, some would argue that the disputational approach favoured by the participants militates against the wider purpose (national, regional and local interests) and in favour of a far narrower purpose (political-party point-scoring).
- Cumulative talk. This is common in settings where the aim is to let people express their feelings or opinions. Examples include therapeutic and counselling contexts. A common place where cumulative talk is found in schools is in PSHE lessons. The process involves participants having their contributions repeated and confirmed by those with whom they are talking. This is a

means of validation, indicating an acceptance of what has been said. It also shows the listener has heard the person's comments and is happy to take them on board. Cumulative talk often involves the elaboration of ideas, either by the original speaker (perhaps at the invitation of a fellow participant) or by someone else with whom the original comment has struck a chord.

- Exploratory talk. This involves participants being critical and constructive. The group has a shared sense of purpose – namely the exploration of a topic in order to further members' knowledge and understanding. As such, there is an air of intellectual endeavour about the talk. Contributions do not gain automatic acceptance (as in cumulative talk), nor are they stated for the purposes of competition (as in disputational talk). Rather, participants make comments which they hope will further understanding. The group explore and assess these in light of a shared set of criteria. In the classroom, these will usually concern notions of reasonableness, logic, evidential support and rationality.

The three types of talk each have their uses. Disputational talk can be rewarding for all involved when it is couched in a formal structure such as that of debating. Cumulative talk is the default option for PSHE, where the teacher's purpose is different to that of most other lessons.

Exploratory talk, however, has the greatest use. It encourages the skills of analysis, synthesis and evaluation, as well as providing a setting in which students can work together in order to achieve a shared goal (greater understanding). Most of the activities in this book promote exploratory talk and many of the strategies and techniques provide means by which to facilitate it. A good way to quickly assess whether or not a discussion in your classroom is exploratory is to bring the two words 'critical' and 'constructive' to mind. If these can be used to describe the kind of talk which is taking place, then you know you are on the right lines.

Three Theorists – Lev Vygotsky

Lev Vygotsky was a Russian psychologist who died in the 1930s. His ideas have had a considerable influence on Western education in recent decades. We will touch briefly on three aspects of his thought here, connecting each to the use of discussion in the classroom.

One of Vygotsky's most well-known concepts is that of the zone of proximal development (ZPD). This is the idea that a child can develop beyond its present, independent capacities, with the help of adult guidance. It is like saying that one can get so far on one's own, but that support is needed to get further. Modelling and scaffolding, two major parts of contemporary pedagogy, are underpinned by this notion.

Teachers who include discussion in their pedagogy can use the ZPD in two distinct ways. First, through their orchestration and modelling of discussion (extended to include such aspects as the interrogation of ideas and the questioning of assumptions) they can help students to move beyond the levels of analysis, synthesis and evaluation they are able to achieve on their own. Second, more able students can offer guidance (either explicitly or implicitly) to the rest of the class through the contributions they make. The teacher can take advantage of this through careful grouping and by calling attention to student responses, demonstrating why that which has been said ought to be deemed as good.

The second aspect of Vygotsky's work we should consider is the relationship he identified between speech and thought. He noted that both inner speech and the speech which we make audible play a considerable role in the development of our conceptual understanding. In each case, it is the use of language which is central. By talking in your 'mind' or by talking with another person, you are manipulating language in order to articulate that which you think.

This process is developmental in the sense that, upon having made an articulation, you have created some form of representation which is your own, and that you are able to assess in light of what you were trying to do (Is that what I meant?). In short, speaking causes one to manipulate language and to think about language. In so doing, and in trying to frame one's thoughts through language, conceptual development takes place. Discussion ought to play an important role in any teacher's pedagogy for this reason alone.

The final idea to which we will turn is that of the child's cultural context. The translated title of one of Vygotsky's key works on education – *Mind and Society* – indicates his view that learning is a social process and that any analysis of learning must take account of the fact that the child exists with and in a context, not as a separate, hermetic entity.

Adults teach children about different aspects of culture. Incorporated in this education are the many tools which humans have developed over time. These include things such as numbers, remembering and maps. The key tool, however, is language, the mastery of which gives the individual the power to do many things both in relation to themselves and in relation to the society of which they are a part. The link to discussion is clear. Through use of the method, teachers are helping students to develop their ability to manipulate language and are teaching them about a variety of tools which are central to our society (for example, analysing other people's speech, constructing arguments and manipulating ideas which one has heard).

These three aspects of Vygotsky's thought, while touched on only briefly here, provide a pedagogical rationale for using discussion, as well as a series of reference points to refer to throughout one's professional practice. I have come back to them myself many times while teaching and planning in order to reaffirm and redirect what it is that I am doing, and what it is that I am asking students to do. Perhaps you will find them equally useful in your own work.

CHAPTER TWO

Strategies and Techniques

In this chapter we consider twenty strategies and techniques which can be used to facilitate excellent discussion and outstanding teaching and learning.

1. Might

Consider the following two questions:

1. What is the answer?
2. What might the answer be?

The meaning of the sentence is significantly altered by the use of the word 'might'. In sentence (1) there is an implied presumption that the questioner knows the answer and expects the person answering to be able to give a response which fits with this. It is akin to asking someone to guess what you are thinking.

In sentence (2) there is an implied presumption that the questioner expects the person answering to use reasoning in their response. The word 'might' signals possibility. In sentence (2) the suggestion is that a number of possible answers may exist and it is for the person asking the question and the person answering the question to explore these. This exploration will include the analysis of answers in relation to a set of criteria (namely, reasoning, evidence and examples given in support of various claims).

In sentence (1) there is a closing down of possibilities. The use of the word 'is' implies the notion of prior existence and the concept of oneness. The question suggests there is a single answer which exists and that, by necessity, this is therefore the correct answer. For some situations in which facts are being checked or ascertained, such a formulation may be appropriate:

a. What is the capital of France?
b. Who is this?
c. What is the answer to the question: Where is the Forth Bridge?

France has only one capital, a person happens to be who they are and only who they are, and the Forth Bridge spans the Firth of Forth in Scotland.

If we take a closer look, however, we may find that, despite appearances, these questions actually afford more than one possible answer:

a. Paris; the administrative centre of the country; the letter 'F'; it depends on the time period to which one is referring; the centre of government.
b. A specific person (Bob Smith); a policeman (who also happens to be Bob Smith); my brother (Bob Smith, a policeman); a criminal (my brother Bob Smith, the corrupt policeman); to me, that person no longer exists (my disgraced brother Bob Smith, a corrupt policeman who the family have excommunicated).
c. In Scotland; north-west of Edinburgh; suspended above the Firth of Forth; just south of Dunfermline; in between North Queensferry and Queensferry

A number of issues are thrown up by this, not least of which is the relative vagueness of language. As teachers, we run the risk of assuming that our own viewpoint is shared by the students we teach. This assumption leads to us mistaking things which are said for that which we think has been said.

A classic example of this is when a student correctly guesses an answer and the teacher assumes that they understand the reasoning which leads to that answer being correct. In actual fact the teacher has no information on which to make a judgement. They must elicit more than the answer itself if they are to have any knowledge of from where it came and whether or not it accords with what the teacher deems to be correct.

Imagine that a particular answer to a particular question is, in the teacher's mind, a small branch at the top of a large, ancient tree. The answer is wholly dependent on everything which came before it. The teacher asks a question akin to formulation (1) outlined above. A student gives an answer which accords with the branch. To all intents and purposes it appears to be identical to the branch. There is no evidence, however, that the branch is at the top of a large, ancient tree. It could be a branch which has been broken off the tree and now lies on the floor. It could be a branch which is being waved in the air by a child. It could be a papier-mâché model of a branch which has been painted so as to look real.

When posing questions to students it is well worth inserting the word 'might'. Doing so consistently is likely to alter the atmosphere of your classroom in the following ways:

- It will make it clear to students that their perspectives are welcome.
- It will show that reasoning is being prioritised over simply giving an answer which accords with what is correct (the most powerful answer is one which is correct because of the reasoning by which it is underpinned).
- It will give students a sense of ownership; the message is that knowledge is being constructed and everybody in the classroom is able to play a part.
- It will encourage students to speculate and to use their own thinking skills in order to put forward possible answers. This is in contrast to the 'what is it?' formulation which can put students off because they fear being wrong.
- It will indicate that, in many situations, a range of interpretations are possible and that these should accord with a set of criteria, rather than being a restatement of what is in the teacher's head (these criteria may be: reason; evidence and examples; originality; 'fit'; or something else).

The implications for discussion are clear. Using the word 'might' opens up a range of possible paths which might be put forward, explored and debated. Maintaining a closed formulation sacrifices this in favour of a misguided belief that the finding of the correct answer is the aim of teaching. It is not. It is one of the aims. More important is the teaching of *how* to find an answer which is correct. Through repeated experience of discursive reasoning students are likely to come to understand the logical formulas, modes of analysis and relationships to evidence that strong, persuasive interpretations or arguments require.

If there are specific facts which students need to know, tell them what they are (or ask them to find out) and then ask them to *do* something with them.

For example, in a lesson on gravity you could begin by explaining what gravity is and at what rate objects fall, both on the Earth and on the Moon. The follow-up question could be: Why might the rate of fall be different on the Earth from what it is on the Moon? This gives students an opportunity to think and discuss, not an opportunity to guess or stay silent. It may be the case that no one puts forward an answer which is correct. However, this will in itself be valuable, because you and the class will be able to analyse the suggestions and demonstrate why they are not correct (perhaps due to faulty reasoning, lack of evidence or counter-examples sufficient to disprove what has been suggested). Finally, if need be, you can explain the correct answer, but do so in a way which makes the reasoning explicit (mirroring the process in which the pupils have engaged).

Using 'might' does not mean descending into relativism (where all answers are equal). Nor is it an excuse to remove the onus on the teacher to teach. Rather, it is a means of opening up discussion and encouraging students to reason. In so doing, it provides a powerful aid to learning.

2. Assigning Group Roles

One of the difficulties inherent to group discussion is the teacher's ceding of control. This can result in students using the opportunity to talk socially or to do no work. Another potential pitfall is that the group may start well but then lose its way. This could be for a number of reasons, including:

◆ One or more members of the group become bored and decide to disengage or to distract other group members.

◆ One or more members of the group encounter intellectual difficulties with the work. This leads them to disengage or to distract other group members.

- The instructions for the activity lack clarity. This leads to ambiguity about what is expected. Students therefore disengage from the task.
- The discussion is truncated due to lack of engagement, deliberate sabotage or a misguided belief that the aim is to finish as quickly as possible.
- Members of the group encounter role difficulties. For example, two members want to lead the group and neither will back down, leading to conflict. Or, no one wishes to lead the group and silence or stop-start discussion follows.

There are three elements which go to make up group discussion:

1. That which is to be discussed and, if stated, the manner in which it is to be discussed.
2. Those who are to be involved in the discussion.
3. The relationships between those who are to be involved in the discussion.

The teacher can deal with the first of these by minimising ambiguity, giving explanations and modelling. The second and third can be dealt with by assigning group roles.

This involves giving students roles to fulfil while they are engaged in discussion. Every member of a group may be given a role, or just a select few. The decision will be determined by the teacher's knowledge of their students. They will use this to help decide which option is most likely to bring about success.

Roles provide a further layer of structure to discussion (beyond the structure provided by the topic and, if appropriate, the manner in which that topic is to be discussed). They help minimise the likelihood of any problems occurring.

Giving students something which it is their job to do creates a sense of responsibility and duty. It is harder to disengage from a discussion if such expectations are incumbent upon you. Also, the roles provide a definite point upon which students can fall back if they become uncertain or unsure of what they are meant to be discussing, or what the discussion is about. The roles provide a safety-net which can catch students before they become disengaged or distracted.

Many possible roles can be assigned. It is best to keep to a small number at first. Pupils can then become familiar with these and what they mean in terms of behaviour. It is also important that roles are rotated over time. Students can become frustrated (rightfully) if they are given the same role over and over again.

One option is to create a set of role-cards, which include short explanations, and to hand these out at the start of a group discussion task. This gives students a reference point to which they can continually refer.

Here is a selection of roles, complete with explanations:

Time-Keeper: It is this person's job to keep track of time. They must ensure that the group completes all the work in the allotted time. They will need to keep the group informed of how much time is left and indicate when it is necessary to move on.

Scribe: It is this person's job to take notes on what is discussed. They should not try to write everything down. Instead, they should try to note down the main ideas and the general points which come out of the discussion.

Leader: It is this person's job to lead the group. They should keep people focussed on the task, ensure everybody gets an opportunity to speak and move the discussion on if necessary.

Devil's Advocate: It is this person's job to challenge the ideas and arguments that people put forward. They should do this by suggesting the opposite of what has been said, looking at things from a completely different viewpoint or by giving counter-examples.

Stingray: It is this person's job to challenge the rest of the group's thinking by making original and unusual contributions. This person should look at the topic and the comments people make from a different perspective to everyone else in the group. This will help them to challenge other people's thinking.

Midwife: It is this person's job to help other people explain their ideas. They should ask questions such as: What do you mean by that? Could you give an example which will explain that? How might you explain your idea slightly differently?

Gadfly: It is this person's job to keep picking away at the discussion. They should ask questions which ensure people are making accurate and precise contributions. They should not let people get away with generalisations, wild comments or things which are vague or unclear.

Demander: It is this person's job to demand reasons, evidence and examples from other group members. If someone makes a claim or an assertion and does not provide sufficient support, the demander must press them to develop their argument until it is stronger and more persuasive.

Observer: This person does not contribute to the discussion. It is their job to observe the discussion and to give feedback when it is completed. This feedback could be to the group and could concern how individual members contributed and how the group worked as a whole. Alternatively, it could be to the class and could concern what was said and the types of arguments and evidence which were used.

Motivator: It is this person's job to motivate their fellow group members. They should maintain a positive attitude and communicate this to the group. If anybody becomes disengaged or unfocussed, the motivator should try to get them back on track.

With all these roles, save that of observer and, in some cases, that of scribe, it is expected that students contribute to the main discussion at the same time as they fulfil their roles.

3. Wait-Time

'Who are you? What do you want? What are you doing here?'

The questions came like water from a dam. Tom was at a loss. His brain was firing in three directions all at once. He looked startled; his mouth was open and his head was gently shaking. The questioner let loose another volley:

'Come on, come on, I haven't got all day. Why are you here? Where have you come from? Who sent you?'

He didn't take a breath as he spat the words out in quick succession. They were accompanied by a venomous stare and the impatient drumming of fingers on the glass table top.

Tom remained rooted to the spot trying to work out what he should say. Barely twenty seconds had passed but it felt like an age. He was swimming in questions; fighting against the tide; looking desperately for a driftwood-answer he could reach out and grab, cling onto for a moment's rest.

'Er…' he said, still trying to form a response, eyes looking up to the ceiling and fingers interlocking.

The drumming got louder. The questioner was working up into a crescendo. A juddering bass-drum crash sounded as he slapped his hand on the table.

'That's it! You've had your time. If you haven't got anything to say then you can get out. My time costs money – and you're wasting it.'

His outstretched forefinger pointed at the door. The three knuckles beneath it were half-framed by luminescent gold. His face was pinched and red. A vein was throbbing at his temple.

Tom followed the imaginary path emanating from the finger with his eyes. He saw the door. His shoulders fell forward and he shuffled to the exit.

Stood outside the room he composed himself. He breathed deeply, ran his hands through his hair and re-buttoned his jacket. He passed down the hallway and entered the lift. At the reception he thanked the secretary and exited through the revolving door. Standing on the stone steps of the office block in which his father worked, the vast steel and glass leviathan rising up behind him, he reflected on the fact that the man in the room would continue in his ignorance and that, for Tom at least, this might just be for the best.

In many situations we advise our students to take time:

'Don't rush it.'

'Take as long as you need.'

'This isn't a race.'

'It's about producing the highest quality work, not finishing first.'

'Slow down.'

Intrinsic to all these comments is the knowledge that acting at speed is liable to lead to worse outcomes than if one takes a little longer and goes about things a little slower. This was exemplified in our fictional extract above.

Here are some of the risks which come from too fast a pace:

- Speed becomes the end in itself, as in those situations where pupils race one another to finish a piece of work, with no regard to the respective quality of the completed items.
- Failure to pay sufficient attention to what the task requires. In these situations, pupils make assumptions based on what they think the task is, rather on what they know it is, having analysed it carefully. This leads to incorrect or flawed results.
- Failure to consider the range of possibilities or influences which may play into or stem from something. It may be that a student who tries to race through a task will produce work which lacks perspective. It could also be that hasty behaviour leads to unintended consequences. For example, stating in an introduction that you will do many different things and then realising later on that it is simply not possible given the situation.

We generally caution students against acting too quickly and praise the benefits of thinking before doing. The underlying message is that thought requires a little time but that the advantages which accrue are far in excess of any costs.

Despite knowing the benefits of not rushing in, and frequently communicating this to students, many teachers nonetheless struggle to apply their own wisdom in the context of whole-class discussions. It is not uncommon for them to ask students questions and to expect an immediate answer. If one is not forthcoming, they often press, ask further questions, or move on to another student. Clearly this is not particularly helpful.

It is of greater benefit to wait. This gives students time to think. In this time they can consider the question or topic under discussion and thus formulate a response which accurately communicates their thoughts regarding the matter. The process of piecing together disparate ideas and synthesising these into clear, articulate speech requires at least a few moments. For many pupils it will require slightly longer.

There are two ways in which to introduce wait-time into your practice. First, after you ask a question, simply wait. If you find this difficult (because you are not used to it), try counting to ten in your head before you speak again. If you count fast then go up to twenty or thirty! Second, after you ask a question, say to the class something along the lines of: 'OK, twenty seconds silent thinking and then we'll share some ideas'.

In both examples you will be providing students with space in which to think about what has been asked, space in which to develop an answer which accurately reflects what is in their minds. Questions and discussion are intended to promote thinking. If it takes a little bit of time, then so be it.

Perhaps one of the greatest difficulties teachers have with implementing wait-time is getting past the feeling that, in a discussion, silence is a bad thing. There are times when silence in discussion creates an awkward feeling. Equally, there are moments when it feels like nothing is happening and no learning is taking place. These feelings need to be ridden out. They must be subjugated to the more important point: it is not speaking alone which creates knowledge and furthers learning in discussion activities. It is speaking combined with thinking. And thinking can take time.

4. Demonstrating Interest and Giving Praise

We will look at demonstrating interest first, and at giving praise second.

There are many boring moments in a teacher's career: meetings, marking, invigilation, data-input and report-writing all come in for regular criticism in the staff room. Much of the job's enjoyment comes from preparing and teaching lessons. In the former case there are creative, intellectual and productive elements and in the latter case these are joined by social and emotional elements.

All these elements are part of the good life: creating things; thinking about and being stimulated by ideas; making something from nothing; doing a duty and providing service; feeling the ebb and flow of emotion, both good and bad; communicating with others. It is the planning and teaching, the actual interaction with students, which draws many into the profession and which sustains many through what can be, at times and like most of life, an up and down ride.

With that said, boredom can work its way into the classroom as well. It can creep up on the teacher as if from nowhere or it can wend its way slowly, and in full view, from a long way off. If one is teaching the same topic year after year, the umpteenth assertion of the same weakly argued position can be akin to the tolling of the bell. It can feel like one's life is slipping away, the lessons merging into an undifferentiated mass and the years weaving together into one indistinguishable bulk. Such experiences can test even the hardiest, most optimistic teacher. They can suck the enthusiasm out of you in a trice.

You must guard against this! Lack of interest is the absolute anathema of discussion. If the teacher is not showing signs of life then why should the students? If what is being debated does not feel vital or, at the least important, then, really, is there any point carrying on with it? You know yourself from sitting through meetings how dispiriting a lack of purpose and a marked indeterminacy about aims can be.

Demonstrating your interest in what students have to say will make them feel good. It will make the whole discussion seem more purposeful and alive; it will allow you to model exemplary behaviour for your students; it will present you with opportunities to probe ideas and to press for further explanation. It gives you the chance to be the energy in the room and to set your pupils' imaginations alight. It allows you to draw in the disengaged and to weave something out of nothing until such a point that your own interest has infected every corner of the classroom and no one has been able to escape the fact that, actually, something really good is going on here.

Don't be patronising; demonstrate genuine interest. If you are not interested in what students are saying then pretend you are. That is part of the job. Remember that for them, if not for you, it is the first time. Think back to what it was like for you when you first encountered new ideas. Focus on the form of what they are saying if you are struggling to show enthusiasm for the content. Ask them about the reasons, evidence and examples they have to support what they are proposing. Ask them to repeat their point more concisely. Ask them how what they are saying connects to something else. Find ways to demonstrate interest. The more you do it, the easier it gets. And the more you do it, the better the discussions in your classroom will be.

Let us now move on to giving praise.

These two strategies are placed together because they both centre on the teacher's social and emotional interactions with students. It is important to remember that teaching, for all its focus on the communication of knowledge and developing of understanding, is predicated not on ideas, things and means, but on the relationships between individuals. A simple way to envisage this is to think of the way in which a class of students can alter its behaviour dramatically when the usual teacher is ill and a substitute has taken their place. Another is to consider the difference between a class at the start of the year and one mid-way through. The relationships between teachers and students underpin much of what happens in the classroom.

Giving praise is a fundamental part of developing good relationships. It makes pupils feel at ease; it shows that you are acknowledging what they have done *and* that you think this is good; it involves the ego in a positive sense; it reinforces that thing which has been praised, encouraging students to repeat the behaviour; it reflects well on you, painting you in a good light in the eyes of students; it creates a nice atmosphere; it douses bad feeling and makes it harder to sustain disengagement; it indicates that you care about what students are doing in your class; it minimises ambiguity by making clear what sort of things are being looked for (those which are praised) and what sort of things are being ignored or admonished.

All these benefits are helpful when a teacher is using discussion. There are two more advantages, however, which are specific to discussion activities. First, by giving praise you are encouraging students to continue taking part in these types of tasks; speaking in front of the class, or even in front of a small group, can be daunting for many pupils. By following what they say with approbation you are putting a little bit on the opposite side of the scales. These students may never be completely at ease with talking in front of others, but the giving of praise on your part will help them to feel more at ease.

Second, praise can be used to demonstrate to the rest of the class what students have done well. This type of praise is the most effective. It requires the teacher to praise an element of a speaker's contribution and to explain why it should be judged as good. Here is an example:

Student: In my opinion, the reason why the British government passed the Great Reform Act of 1867 was because they knew it would not include much redistribution of seats but would appease the British public who had been agitating for reform.

Teacher: Excellent comment, thank you. What I particularly liked was that you provided detailed reasoning to support your view. You connected two points together in order to show how they supported the opinion you put forward.

Such interactions do not always need to be so long. Nor is detailed exposition always required. The key is to continually identify the specific things, related to the learning, for which praise is being given. Such an approach benefits the student who is receiving praise, as well as the class as a whole. It will also lead to higher quality discussion as students seek to mimic that which has been identified as good.

5. Ground Rules

Life is beset by rules. As adults we implicitly know, acknowledge and act in accordance with these. Many students make the complaint that school life is riddled with rules. An alternative interpretation is that because the great majority of individuals in a school (the students) are inexperienced in operating successfully in society the rules need to be more visible and more explicit. Further support for this argument is provided by the fact that many rules in school echo the kind of behaviour which is taken for granted in adult life. Much of this is behaviour concerned with interactions, although some of it is focussed on the individual's relationship with themselves (though this, in turn, can influence their relations with others).

Rules in schools, and many other institutions, tend to come in three separate forms:

- Fixed written rules
- Fixed verbal rules
- Unstated but implied rules

It is fair to say that free-floating verbal rules can exist but these are infrequent and are usually the mark of poor thought, bad planning or an autocratic bent. If a rule is not fixed it becomes difficult to follow and loses its function as an external reference point for the community. Instead, it is bound to the whim of the individual, group or organisation that has the power to alter it and to enforce sanctions in accordance with its being broken.

The argument then is that in school students are learning the rules (of the school and, by extension, of society) and that the rules are being used for regulation of the community, primarily the interactions within that community. One area of conflict which can develop is between different groups who perceive the reasoning behind rules differently. Such interpretations are often informed by wider worldviews, with these usually being predicated on moral judgements and the prioritisation, whether made explicit or not, of certain values.

So, for example, a secondary school may introduce a rule which states that any student who arrives late will automatically receive a half hour detention on that same day. The school may justify this rule by pointing to the benefit to the child of not being late, the expectation of punctuality in the workplace and society at large, and the disruption which lateness causes to the community (in the form of students arriving late to lessons). A parent who believes that the primary function of a school is to provide a safe and welcoming environment for their child may dispute the validity of the rule. They may argue that such a measure is draconian and potentially disproportionate. They may cite examples such as lateness caused by unavoidable incidents (like a road traffic accident which has led to major delays). Their case may conclude on the emotive note that a rule such as this diminishes the positive feelings their child has towards school and creates a punitive climate akin to less desirable types of institution.

This example illustrates the way in which different people's standpoints can profoundly influence their perception of rules and the reasoning behind them, as well as how they go about interpreting them.

In a moment we will draw this exposition back to using discussion in the classroom; however, one more point is worthy of note. Let us consider a few rules which are common to most schools and which tend to be stated in fixed written form and reiterated by staff members (and, sometimes, students) in fixed verbal form:

1. Do not run in the corridors.
2. Treat others with respect.
3. Follow the teacher's instructions.

Rule (1) is concerned with the health and safety of individuals and the community. It is also concerned with atmosphere and ethos as well as the demarcating of space (if you want to run, go outside). Rule (2) is primarily focussed on interactions between individuals. It is about as broad as a rule could get without becoming meaningless. It encompasses all individuals who happen to be in the school at any time (staff, students and visitors). It could be argued that there is an implied reference to the permanent members of the community and that a visitor is a special case who becomes a member of the community for the period during which they are in school. Rule (3) is a power-giving rule which supplements the teacher's own methods of asserting control in the classroom. It regulates behaviour between teacher and students but also between any particular student and the peers with whom they share a class. It is implied in the rule that the teacher's instructions will be in the pupils' best interests (or, perhaps, the school's best interests). If not, it would be a perverse rule.

We have, then, a collection of points about rules in school:

1. They tend to be more visible and more explicit in schools than in society at large.
2. They reflect standards of accepted and expected behaviour in wider society.
3. They come in different forms but are usually fixed.
4. They can be interpreted and perceived differently. Multiple viewpoints can be equally valid.
5. They have different purposes. A common one is the regulation of behaviour.
6. They act as external reference points for the community.

Points (2), (5) and (6) indicate why it is of great benefit to have ground rules underpinning the discussion activities taking place in your classroom. Point (4) suggests why you should seek to agree your ground rules with your class at the beginning of the year. Point (3) implies how the rules should be formulated and connects closely to point (6).

You may choose to write your ground rules down and display them in your classroom. You may choose to reiterate them verbally throughout the year (this can include the identification and subsequent praise of rule-following behaviour). You may choose to build an atmosphere in which the rules are known but not articulated. Whichever method you choose, your life will be easier, your discussions will be better and your students will know where they stand and what is expected of them.

6. Bouncing

Most classrooms have the following structure:

- One teacher who spends most of the time at the front of the room either stood up or sat down. They may also move around the room (circulate) so as to look at students' work, so as to talk to individual students, or in order to use non-verbal means of behaviour management.
- A number of students, often between fourteen and thirty, but always outnumbering the teacher, who will usually spend most of the time sitting down, unless: (i) it is a Drama, Physical Education or Design and Technology lesson; (ii) the lesson involves a practical, such as in a Science lesson; or (iii) the teacher is using activities which specifically involve movement.
- At the front of the room there is a means of displaying information. In most British schools today this is in the form of an interactive whiteboard. It could also be a traditional whiteboard, a blackboard or an overhead projector.

This structure commonly results in the teacher standing at the front of the room, conveying information to their students. Pupils, in turn, switch their attention between the teacher and the information being displayed.

The least effective form of this method sees the teacher talking at length, with students being expected to ingest and assimilate that which is said and that which is shown. The approach treats the human mind like a bucket and imagines that the teacher's job is to fill up the bucket.

The most effective form of this method sees the teacher talking for a short period of time in order to explain what the students are then going to do, or talking a little longer in order to develop a teaching point (with subsequent indication of what the students are expected to do with that teaching point). In this case, the use of the method is premised on the fact that mass communication can be used to set the class off on an activity in which they actively engage with whatever they are learning about.

Common to both approaches is the structural relationship which exists in the classroom whereby the teacher is at the front, with the ability to stand up and sit down at will, while the students fan out from near the front to the back and are not allowed to stand up unless given express permission.

Personally, I have no problem with this arrangement. While I think it is good to change the room layout from time to time in order to facilitate different types of activities, I feel that this traditional set-up is easily the most practicable and, as long as it is not viewed uncritically and as long as excessive teacher talk is avoided, it provides a simple structure which deals with the numerical imbalance between teacher and students very effectively. The reason I have brought it up here, however, is because of a particular behaviour it promotes in whole-class discussion.

That behaviour is the narrowing of debate, such that it becomes a repetitive cycle of teacher-student interactions. This involves the teacher posing a question, a student responding, the teacher responding to what has been said, another or the same student responding to the teacher's comment and so on; a back-and-forth dynamic in which all exchanges go through the teacher.

The traditional layout of the classroom is more likely to engender this situation. The teacher, standing at the front, asks the whole class (all of whom they can see) a question. Students, who are all looking at the teacher, think of a response. The teacher picks out a student. They respond, talking back to the teacher (as is natural and polite – addressing the person who has spoken). The teacher comments on this because that is also polite. They then return the discussion to the class by picking another student. And on it goes.

Such behaviour risks diminishing the efficacy of whole-class discussion for the following reasons:

1. The flow of the discussion is stifled. It becomes formulaic due to the repeated imposition of the teacher's voice and thoughts.

2. It is harder for students to comment on what other students have said because all student-comments are compressed between teacher-comments.

3. A single discussion is not really taking place. Instead, there are a series of mini-discussions between the teacher and individual students. The rest of the class listen to these.

A simple way to avoid these pitfalls and to encourage student-student interactions (a mix of student-student and teacher-student interactions, weighted in favour of the former is probably ideal) is through the technique of bouncing.

Imagine that the discussion is a ball which is passed from one speaker to the next. Instead of accepting the ball from a student, seek to pass it on to another student. Here is how:

Student A: So, in my opinion, I think long prison sentences are good because they deter people from committing crimes.

Teacher: An interesting idea. Student B, do you agree with Student A's opinion?

Student B: Well, I'm not sure that they do deter people, because if you commit a crime it might just be in the heat of the moment and you wouldn't have time to think about prison sentences.

[At this point it is clear that Student A wants to respond. The teacher makes a non-verbal signal for them to do so.]

Student A: Yeah, I take your point, but if they know that there are long prison sentences, then even in the heat of the moment there will be something in their mind telling them that they're taking a big risk.

[A third student, Student C, has put their hand up. The teacher indicates that they can speak next.]

Student C: Long prison sentences make the public feel better; they're not really about putting people off crime because people are going to commit crime anyway.

This technique – of bouncing the discussion to another student – sees the teacher as a facilitator rather than a leader.

It takes time to develop the skill. Sometimes a series of bounces can lead to no responses. You must develop your judgement about when to step in and redirect the discussion or when to recapitulate what has been said. It may be preferable to maintain teacher-student interactions in classes where behaviour is difficult. As is evident from the sample dialogue though, bouncing leads to discussions which are more engaging for students and which promote active learning.

7. Modelling Discussion

As the teacher, students are watching you and analysing how you behave. They will act in accordance with what they observe. If you model excellent discussion you are setting an example for them; you are giving them something to follow, something to mimic, something to take on board and make their own. Here are ten areas in which you can model great discussion:

Manners

Civility should to permeate all our interactions. Whether we are engaged in a debate over the relative merits of some position, a discussion regarding a topic of interest, or a dialogue concerning the nature of some abstract concept, we should seek to display good manners. Model this for your students. Be scrupulous in thanking them for their contributions. Apologise if you misrepresent somebody, speak over them or accidently fail to bring them into the conversation. Maintain a posture which demonstrates attentiveness. Smile where appropriate. Avoid interrupting people. If there are rules, observe them.

Reasoning

Classroom discussions should promote good reasoning and challenge that which is bad. Reasoning is sound if there is a logical connection between the propositions and the conclusion. Reasoning is bad if the propositions do not cohere with the conclusion or if fallacies are invoked and treated as if they were logically sound. When you contribute to discussion you should ensure that your arguments are built on good reasoning. You should explain to students why your reasoning is good. You should also demonstrate why bad reasoning is bad, if the opportunity arises (though do it in such a way as to take account of the speaker's feelings. Do not waver, but do not go in too hard).

Giving Evidence

Evidence is that which is known to exist in the world or ideas or concepts which are accepted as reputable according to a given set of criteria (often discipline specific). Taking Sociology as an example, a student discussing crime could call on evidence in the form of the British Crime Survey (which records things which have happened in the world) or the concept of labelling (which sociologists in general agree is an accurate theorisation of a real-world occurrence). When you make contributions to class discussion, be sure to provide relevant evidence to support your arguments. In the process, explain to students what your evidence is and why it is apt.

Giving Examples

An example provides a reference point for an abstract idea. It demonstrates the understanding of the person who is giving the example and offers support for whatever is being asserted. Here is an example(!):

(a) Gladstone was what we would call today a 'conviction politician'. (b) For example, his campaigning from 1876 onwards was based on his opposition to the Bulgarian atrocities. This was, for him, a deeply moral issue.

Part (a) is the abstract idea. Part (b) is the example. It provides support for (a) by indicating how (a) might be seen as manifest in the real world. It also demonstrates the author's knowledge of some of the history of Gladstone's political career (this being necessary in order for the claim (a) to be regarded as worthy of consideration).

Give examples when you are contributing to class discussions for the reasons stated above. Also, identify when students have given examples and demonstrate why what they have said is desirable.

Listening

Throughout a whole-class discussion, the vast majority of participants will be – or ought to be – listening. If more than one person is talking then the discussion is in danger of disintegrating. At such a point the teacher needs to reassert control, wait for silence and then return to the person whose turn it was to talk. One of the best ways to encourage listening is through modelling. When a student is speaking, look at them and concentrate on what they are saying. Make it absolutely clear to other students in the class that this is what you are doing and that it is what you expect them to be doing as well. If you model attentive, focussed listening it is also easier to admonish (where necessary) students who are failing to listen.

Asking Questions

When someone speaks we will not by necessity understand all that they say. Nor will we necessarily be struck dumb by their eloquence (though it does happen on occasion). For both these reasons we may feel the need to ask them questions. Modelling this process is good because it not only shows how to go about asking thoughtful questions but it also demonstrates that you have been listening. The two key types of questions to ask are questions of clarification (What do you mean by that? How does that connect to the topic?) and questions which probe what has been said (Do you think that would still hold in context X? Why might someone disagree with that position?). Modelling such questioning should eventually lead your students to do it without any prompting.

Remaining Silent

This has been touched on above but deserves to be treated separately. It is polite to remain silent while someone else is talking. In the classroom, it is also unjust to speak during a discussion when it is not your turn. This is because the individual who does so prevents the whole class from learning and participating. They are thus privileging their own desires above the good of the community. Of course, there are times when an interruption or comment may be better dealt with by the teacher drawing it into the discussion rather than chiding the speaker. Overall though, the best path is to model silence and to encourage turn-taking.

Looking at the Speaker

Often, students may not realise how rude it can be to look around the room while someone is making a contribution to a discussion. It is important to model looking at the speaker in order to make it clear that this is the correct way to behave. A brief exposition may be given as a supplement, pointing to the respect it demonstrates and the fact that it is done for the benefit of the person speaking as much as anyone else (students often make the claim that they are listening and therefore do not need to look as well).

Showing Interest

This was dealt with in an earlier section. It is included here because showing interest is not only beneficial to the speaker and to the maintenance of a positive atmosphere, but it also models such behaviour for students. The expectation is that pupils will follow the example the teacher is setting.

Responding to What Has Been Said

This links into asking questions and to listening. Students will frequently want to make their own points during discussions. This is good because it demonstrates interest and shows that they are thinking about the topic. It can mean that what other pupils say is sometimes ignored, though, with pupils instead focussing on their own thoughts. By responding to what students say, and explaining that you are doing it, you can highlight the importance of engaging with the ideas which are being brought into the discussion. In addition, you can model a responsive question or statement but then 'bounce' this out to one or more students. This will result in you modelling while also avoiding excessive teacher talk.

8. Scaffolding

Scaffolding involves the following:

- The teacher helping the student to go further than they would be able to go themselves.
- The teacher helping the student to achieve something more quickly than would be possible if they were left to their own devices.
- The teacher taking a student to a certain point, which they could not have accessed, or would have had difficulty accessing, on their own, before letting them take over.

Here are six examples of scaffolding, two each for paired, group and whole-class discussion.

Paired Discussion

1. Provide each pair with a set of questions or statements related to the topic. Ask them to work through the list, discussing each question or statement in turn. It may be beneficial for students to make a few notes covering what they talk about. These can then be used as memory aids in a subsequent whole-class discussion informed by the work students have done in pairs.

   This method is suggested because some pupils may find it difficult to maintain a discussion about a particular topic. They may not have sufficient understanding of the subject to identify points worthy of discussion. It could be that they have not yet mastered the nature of discussion and cannot sustain unstructured conversation, even when the topic is one which they know a lot about. Alternatively, it might be the case that students struggle, for whatever reason, to get going. The list thus provides a prompt which can be used to get discussion up and running. It can also be returned to for support during the course of the activity.

2. Give pairs some material in which a number of relevant arguments are rehearsed. This could be a newspaper article, a piece of work produced by a student in the previous year, some text from a website, or the transcript of an imaginary discussion which you have written up. Ask pupils to read through the material. When they have finished, provide them with two or three comprehension questions to discuss in their pairs (What is the article about? What arguments are put forward in the text?). The results of this initial discussion can then lead on to a more general discussion of the arguments at issue.

   This method is suggested because it provides students with a range of ideas to use in their discussions at the same time as it gives a lead-in to the main task. The material might cause pupils to think of their own ideas, or it may not. Either way, they will still have something to talk about.

Group Discussion

1. If you have a group of students who are particularly weak in discussion activities (and it is not possible for them to work with pupils who are more skilled, or you have tried this and it has been unsuccessful) then you can try sitting with them and being a full member of their discussion.

   This role is difficult to play. You do not want to take over and you do not want to inhibit the pupils. You are aiming to provide just enough input to make things easier for the group and to continue treading this fine line throughout the task. It is a little like trying to maintain a constant temperature in a bath. Doing too much will cause problems, as will doing too little.

   This method is suggested because it takes the onus of starting and sustaining discussion away from those students who find such tasks difficult. This frees them up to think about the topic. Further, the teacher's interventions can ensure the discussion is steered towards areas about which the teacher knows the students have prior knowledge or existing opinions.

2. Provide each group with a discussion frame. This is a table with two columns. The first column contains words, concepts or phrases linked to the topic under discussion. The second column is left blank. Each group is expected to cover the various words, concepts and phrases in the course of their discussion. One person should be chosen to scribe. They should make notes in the blank column, detailing what was said by members of the group.

   This method is suggested because the frames provide a set of reference points from which groups can begin their discussions. The frames also provide a structure which helps sustain debates over time.

Whole-Class Discussion

1. Precede discussion with the creation of a spider-diagram about the topic. Leave this spider-diagram on the board for the duration of the discussion. It will provide students with a great deal of information which they will be able to revisit during the course of the activity. By pooling the resources of the class

(lots of different students will make contributions to the spider-diagram) and supplementing this with knowledge from the teacher (the students may miss some important issues) a high-level starting point is reached which all pupils are able to access.

This method works particularly well with whole-class discussions because of the visibility of the material. A spider-diagram can be easily constructed on a traditional board as well as on an interactive whiteboard. If there is enough space, you can continue adding to it during the discussion. The teacher could do this, or a student. If the latter, it may be a good task for someone who does not feel confident speaking in class; it is an alternative way for them to be involved.

2. Film yourself and a colleague engaged in a discussion. Produce three short pieces, the first of which exemplifies bad discussion, the second of which shows discussion of a reasonable quality and the third of which demonstrates high-quality discussion. Show these to your students before you start your activity. They will help pupils understand what they need to do in order to discuss well.

The method requires some preparation time. In its favour is the fact that, once you have made the video, you can use it over and over again, year after year. It is akin to modelling and it is fair to say that, in general, the two concepts (modelling and scaffolding) are very close – two branches of the same tree as it were.

A final note before we leave this strategy. The different methods are not exclusive to the type of discussion under which they are listed and can be used or adapted to fit a range of different situations.

9. Pushing Reasoning

Reasoning forms an integral part of discussion. There are some instances – notably when teaching Personal, Social and Health Education (PSHE) – where it is appropriate for students to share their thoughts and opinions without the addition of further support. In most situations, however, contributions which are simply assertions should be followed up on by the teacher. This will indicate to students that, when a topic is at issue, everyone is entitled to their opinion, but not all opinions are equal. Those which are based on sound reasoning, which have evidence to support them, or which are clearly exemplified are stronger, more persuasive opinions than those which have none of these things. Here is an example:

Student A: I like ice-cream.

Student B: I like ice-cream because it tastes nice and comes in a number of attractive colours and flavours.

Student C: I like ice-cream because it tastes nice and comes in a number of striking colours and flavours. The colours, such as bright green, are attractive to the eye and the flavours, such as chocolate, stimulate the senses and release chemicals in the brain.

Student A makes an assertion but offers no support. If they were talking in a social setting this would be fine – we all make statements like this throughout the day. In the context of a classroom discussion the statement has limited validity, though. It is not furthering understanding, seeking to persuade or articulating a thought process. It does not help the group to learn or to become wiser.

Student B offers two reasons to explain why they like ice-cream. These are presented in a connected form and there is an implied suggestion that colours and flavours are intimately linked. There are two unstated premises: (i) Something tasting nice is a good thing and (ii) Variety is a good thing.

Student C develops the reasoning further by going into detail about the nature of the colours and the flavours. They provide reasons as to why they should be seen as good, giving examples in each case. In addition, they give some evidence in the shape of the scientific information concerning the release of chemicals. It could be argued that they also provide evidence in the form of a widely accepted concept – that of attractiveness. This carries the connotations of aesthetics and the idea of beauty. By using 'attractive' in this way, the pupil is appealing to a notion commonly held by many people in the wider community.

Clearly then, Student C's opinion carries more weight than that of either Student A or Student B. Again, this is not to discount their opinions, but it is to draw attention to the fact that reasoning, evidence and examples are key facets of persuasive argument.

When using discussion in the classroom, it is important to push students' reasoning. This does not mean that you should identify a particular style and ask everyone to conform. Nor does it mean that discussions are a competitive search for the best reasoner. Rather, it means that students should come to understand that they will be expected to give reasons, evidence and examples for the points they make and that the teacher will press them to do so. Fostering such a culture in your classroom will be doing your students a great service. It will help them to think more clearly, to speak more persuasively and to write better.

It is worth spending some time talking to students about what good reasoning entails, including the use of appropriate evidence and examples. There are three main types of reasoning, detailed below.

Deductive Reasoning: If A then B. If B then C. Therefore, if A then C. This involves being able to deduce a conclusion from logically prior premises. The classic formulation of this is: All men are mortal. Socrates is a man. Therefore, Socrates is mortal.

Inductive Reasoning: This is reasoning from observation. I notice that the sun has risen every day of my life so far. I reason from this that it will rise tomorrow. A problem with inductive reasoning is that one counter-example can destroy the whole proposition. For example: I see only white swans for the first seventeen years of my life. Throughout that period I work under the assumption that all swans are white – this argument being a result of my experience. On my eighteenth birthday I go to a zoo and see a black swan. My white swan proposition, despite the fact that I have seen hundreds of them over many years, is shattered by this one incident.

Analogical Reasoning: This is reasoning by analogy. It involves making a judgement of similarity. This involves noting that two things share something and that, consequently, they also have other similarities. For example: Society is like the human body. They both have important parts that work in unison yet remain quite different.

In addition to the different types of reasoning, it is worth making students aware of some of the reasons why evidence and examples are important.

- **Evidence:** This provides recognised and accepted support in the form of facts, observations and other such empirical data, or in the form of concepts or theoretical ideas which are held to be true or accurate by a number of people or groups. Empirical evidence proves or disproves theories or hypotheses because these are statements made about the world. The evidence is the data which is collected from observation of, experience of, or experiments involving the world. Therefore, it either holds true for what a statement about the world asserts, or it falsifies it.
- **Examples:** This has been noted elsewhere. Briefly, examples provide a specific real-world reference for an abstract point. They demonstrate that which is being asserted.

These brief summaries are not extensive. Nonetheless, for the purpose of pushing reasoning in discussions they provide sufficient information for teachers and students to think about.

10. Discussion Which Precedes Writing

Discussion is a great way to help students develop their ideas about a topic before they start doing any writing. It gives an opportunity to think at length and to hear the thoughts of others. What is more, because of the fluid nature of speech, students can edit, refine, rehash, delete and alter their views and opinions at will without leaving any traces behind. This is beneficial because, when it comes to writing, students will be able to produce work which has already gone through a drafting process.

It may be suggested that, in this context, discussion is being used as a means to an end, that end being the writing of a high-quality piece of work concerning the topic under consideration. I do not think the contention holds. A discussion which precedes a written task is still an end in itself. The same rules, intentions and expectations of discussion apply and if, for some reason, the written task were to be jettisoned at the last minute, then the learning which had taken place during and because of the discussion would remain valid and could easily stand alone. Suffixing writing to discussion takes advantage of this learning and allows for two separate ends to be achieved: the development of understanding through discussion and the written articulation of understanding.

It is up to you whether or not you signal to students that they will be writing following their discussion. On the one hand, this could cause them to think about the possible implications of their talk for their writing. In addition, it might lead them to take more detailed notes than would otherwise have been the case. On the other hand, indicating that a writing task is to follow could have the effect of inhibiting students. Some may not wish to share their thoughts for selfish reasons while others may struggle to keep their attention on the task in hand.

The method I favour is to indicate to pupils that writing will follow discussion but that both are of equal importance. I also add that the better the discussion the more likely it is that the writing will come easily. Finally, I am careful to not mention the writing again until after the discussion is completed. This serves to avoid turning students' attention away from the task in hand and also stops the discussion being undermined by thoughts about what is to follow.

Using discussion to precede writing requires a little bit of careful planning. First, it is important that you ensure the two tasks are closely connected and that their relationship is clear to students. If not, there is the risk that pupils will get confused during the transition and will not be able to make use of the speaking, listening and thinking work they have done in the first task.

Second, you should give consideration to the relative difficulty levels of the two tasks and the amount of scaffolding they may require. For many students, speaking is easier than writing. As such, you may need to give more support during the written task.

Further, the different demands made by writing may mean that it is not possible to deal with the topic in exactly the same way as was the case during discussion. You will need to decide whether or not the same approach can be used, or if it will need to be altered to fit the different medium.

We will now look at three examples of how discussion might precede writing so as to contextualise the comments made above.

1. The discussion is structured so that different students are asked to argue for different propositions about an issue. This will result in most pupils identifying with the position for which they have advocated while developing an understanding of the various other arguments which exist. The written task can play to these strengths by asking students to defend the position they spoke in favour of, including suitable rebuttals of the other arguments.

2. There is a general discussion about a particular topic in which a number of different issues are explored. For the writing task, the teacher identifies these issues and places them on the board so that the whole class can see them. The teacher explains that students can choose which of the issues they would like to write about. They have the option of picking one and producing an in-depth piece of work or picking a number, each of which they cover in slightly less detail.

3. The discussion is predicated on a question. The debate revolves around this and student contributions are always brought back to it. The overarching aim is to try to answer the question. In the written task, students take the question as their title and are presented with two options. They can either provide an overview of the various points which were put forward or they can write an extended piece arguing for their own point of view. Either way, they will be producing a piece of work which draws on the discussion and which is focussed and structured.

In each of these examples we can see how the two tasks have been intertwined. It is not the case that a discussion activity and a writing task have been tacked together. Rather, they have been moulded so as to ensure a fit which is intellectually sound and which will benefit pupils. There are many other ways in which such a synthesis can be crafted. All, however, will share the same features.

On a final note, it is perfectly possible to have a further discussion after the writing has been completed. This could focus on students' views and how these have been affected by the writing they have done, or it could centre on the quality of the writing itself. This latter option would be a reflective, peer- and self-assessment discussion designed to help students think critically about the work they have produced.

11. Discussion Which Succeeds Writing

Much of what was said in the previous section applies here. Where discussion succeeds writing, both tasks should be seen as ends in themselves. A successful synthesis will involve two activities which are closely connected. The connection should also be easy for students to see. The teacher will need to plan carefully to ensure this is the case.

Three significant advantages stand out regarding the use of discussion after writing. First, by giving students time to write you are giving them time to think. This thinking will be about the topic and so is likely to lead to a more informed discussion. Also, the act of turning one's thoughts on a matter into prose involves a number of processes which aid understanding. These include: synthesis of disparate elements; the identification of connections and differences; the logical sequencing of information; the refining of explanation, argument or description; and the specifying (through language) of internal impressions and sensations.

Second, starting with writing means each student begins by engaging privately and personally with the topic. Discussion, by its nature, is a social activity. It cannot be done alone. Writing, on the other hand, can. The benefit of this to students is that they all get an opportunity to think about the topic without interruption or the input of others. Later on, when discussion ensues, they will share their ideas and be presented with the viewpoints of their peers. This may lead to alterations, agreements, rebuttals and the like. During the period of writing, though, all that is put on hold, allowing students to focus solely on their own thoughts and to determine what exactly they think about the topic in question.

Third, producing a piece of written work means students have something to which they can refer during the discussion. Pupils who struggle to make contributions can use it as a support; it also provides a fall-back option for the teacher if debate dies down (they can ask a student to read out what they wrote and then call for responses).

Here are three examples of how you might use writing to precede discussion:

1. Set students a question or provide a contentious statement which relates to the topic you are studying. Ask them to produce a written response. This could be made easier through

the provision of sentence starters, a suggested structure or a selection of sub-points which a good answer ought to cover. This method will allow students to formulate their thoughts on the issue, meaning they will be in a more advanced position at the start of the discussion than would otherwise have been the case. This will help raise the level of the discussion and is also likely to make students feel more confident about contributing.

2. Put forward a proposition regarding the topic which is being studied. Divide the class in two. Explain that half the class will be writing an argument which is in favour of the proposition and that half the class will be writing one which is against the proposition. Allow students a few minutes to discuss in their two large groups what possible points might be raised in support of their respective positions. After this, pupils should set about writing their arguments independently. The ensuing discussion will be, initially at least, an either/or affair. Once a range of arguments for and against have been debated, the teacher can indicate that students are free to alter their positions if they so wish.

   This method gives students a very clear focus and also introduces a competitive element. It ensures that pupils learn one side of an issue very well, although, because they will also be considering the various ways in which their opponents may seek to rebut their arguments, it should also help them to develop a working knowledge of the other perspective too.

3. Ask students to write a report on an aspect of the topic you are studying. You may decide that all students should focus on the same aspect, or you may decide to hand out a range of different aspects. If you can rely on your pupils, ask them to do this for homework. If you are not confident in it being completed outside of lessons, then set up the activity in class and provide the necessary resources. After sufficient time has elapsed, or at the beginning of the next lesson, begin a debate around your area of study.

   The great advantage of this method is that the report writing will provide pupils with detailed knowledge of the area which is to be discussed. They will be able to talk confidently and accurately about the issue or topic, using their research in order to make points and advance arguments. Their reports can be kept on-hand while the discussion takes place, allowing students to refer to them as and when is necessary. It will also make discussion feel like a business meeting. This dramatic element lends a nice sense of theatricality to proceedings (some pupils may even brandish their reports at their peers!).

Similar to the extension suggested in the previous section, it can be of great use to return to writing immediately after the discussion concludes. Students can rewrite their work in light of what they have said, heard and thought during the discussion. Even if their perspective remains unchanged, they should still be able to supplement their work with further evidence, arguments or rebuttals.

12. Roles of the Teacher

There are many roles which the teacher can take during a discussion. Here are eight useful ones, the first four of which stem from the character of Socrates as depicted in the writings of Plato.

Ignoramus: This involves the teacher 'acting dumb' in order to draw out the thinking which underpins a statement. It should not be done in an ostentatious or overstated manner as this may provoke irritation or come across as patronising. It is appropriate to ask questions such as: 'What do you mean by that?' 'I don't really understand; can you explain that in more detail?' and 'How exactly would that work?' The purpose is to encourage the speaker to elucidate. It is a particularly useful role to play when students are taking things for granted about the audience's knowledge and understanding, making general or blasé statements, or basing their comments on assumptions.

Midwife: This involves the teacher helping pupils to 'give birth' to their ideas. They use questions, prompts and suggestions as aids, teasing the connections, reasoning and examples out of what pupils have initially said. The teacher is providing support to students, pointing and nudging them in the right direction, making use of their extensive knowledge to do so, but all the while being certain to leave it up to the students to do the work. Taking on the role of midwife involves treading a fine line between being gnomic and providing the answer which you believe is coming.

Gadfly: A gadfly is a fly which annoys large animals by biting them before flying away. They may return repeatedly to the same animal, each time inflicting a bite which, while relatively small, is nonetheless annoying and potentially painful. Due to a gadfly's size and agility it is difficult for the animal it is biting to see it off. Taking on the role of a gadfly in discussion involves continually asking questions which undermine statements by picking up on loose reasoning, fallacies, bad evidence and the like. In the classroom, such a role is not designed to irritate students but to encourage them to be more precise and accurate in what they say. It is best played jovially so as to lessen the sting, ensuring that the focus remains on the elements of argument to which the teacher wishes to draw attention.

Stingray: Stingrays have barbed stings on their tails which they use in self-defence. They usually include venom glands and give any recipient a sharp, at times fatal, shock. A literal translation of this would lead to one's teaching career being abruptly cut short. A figurative translation will not. This sees the teacher throwing statements or questions into the discussion which are designed to shock the group in order to make them think differently. For example: in a discussion concerning Hamlet's role in the play of the same name, a teacher taking on the stingray role may shock the group into thinking differently by posing the question: What if Hamlet had been a woman?

Devil's Advocate: The devil's advocate takes on positions antithetical to those being advanced so as to encourage the speaker to improve and strengthen their argument. The purpose is to present an alternative perspective – sometimes near unthinkable, sometimes bizarre or unlikely – which will compel the person proposing an argument to extend their reasoning and to rebut or, if possible, refute the opposing thesis. It is sometimes assumed that the person playing devil's advocate believes in the points they are putting forward. This is often not the case; the devil's advocate is playing a role and invariably seeks to strengthen the arguments underpinning the original proposition.

Facilitator: A facilitator sees their role as essentially procedural. Their job is to ensure that the people who are taking part in the discussion are able to do so successfully. In effect, the facilitator performs a function for the group; they do whatever is necessary to allow the smooth running of the discussion without actually getting involved in it themselves. In the classroom this will include indicating whose turn it is to speak, reminding participants of the ground rules, asking people to repeat their contributions if they have not been heard and so on.

Committed Participant: The role of committed participant requires careful consideration. It involves the teacher stating what they believe and then playing a full part in the discussion, advocating for their beliefs where appropriate. The risks are that they may lose sight of the wider aims and that students may feel overpowered by the teacher's presence. In addition, pupils may agree with the teacher because of the authority they hold, rather than because of the arguments they put forward. On the other hand, making contributions which are genuine and reflect a well-developed perspective can provide an excellent model for students to follow. Also, if the topic is a sensitive one and you are expecting pupils to share their thoughts, taking part yourself can be a good way of encouraging participation while pressing home a sense of equality in the classroom.

Neutral Judge: The neutral judge oversees the debate, using a set of criteria to determine when and when not to intervene. I would suggest the criteria should cover behaviour and thinking. In the former case the teacher will intervene in order to admonish bad behaviour and to praise good behaviour. In the latter case the teacher will intervene to query reasoning or to ask for clarification or expansion of points. It may also be appropriate for the teacher playing the neutral judge to summarise arguments which are made and to make concluding remarks at the end of the activity.

It is likely that in most discussions the teacher will switch between various roles depending on the immediate demands of the debate. Practice leads one to develop an understanding of when a role is best used.

13. Partners First

Discussions often stall at the first stages. This is frequently because students either do not want to say anything or do not feel they have anything worth contributing. We will deal with each point in turn.

At the beginning of a discussion there is a sense of emptiness. There is a void which, if all goes well, will eventually be filled with thoughts, opinions, arguments and ideas. To reach such a point, members of the group will need to contribute; they will need to create the discussion through what they say. A discussion, after all, is simply the sum of the words which are spoken. In this, it is quite different from many of the activities which teachers use in the classroom. Tasks which involve reading, writing, experimenting, acting and creating often have more structure and are less reliant on the contributions which students make. This is not to say those activities will work if the students do not take part – clearly they won't. What it does mean, though, is that those activities will not fail if some students choose not to take part. The remaining students will, in most cases, be able to get on with the task and achieve what the teacher intended.

In a group or whole-class discussion, the teacher needs student involvement in order to achieve their aims. If no one contributes to a discussion then it is not a discussion. If only one or two students contribute then it is debateable how much of a discussion it really is.

At the start, when the emptiness is evident to all, there are a number of social factors at play which militate against student involvement. The first is fear of failure. Speaking in front of a group is something many pupils find intimidating. Once a discussion is up and running this is not a problem; comments are made *as part of the group*. At the beginning, however, contributions are made *to* the group. This is because the discussion itself does not yet exist; it only will once a sufficient number (not many) of comments have been made. So students can have a tendency to feel that they are putting themselves up in front of the group and, in so doing, are putting themselves up for judgement (the implicit argument being that if someone speaks first and speaks to the group then surely they ought to think what they say is right). I believe this feeling is a genuine one for many students but that it is founded on incorrect assumptions. Rarely, if ever, do the first few comments in a discussion provoke any kind of negative response. Rarely, if ever, do students start off with things which could be construed negatively.

The second social factor at play is embarrassment. Students may feel embarrassed for a number of reasons:

1. They may not know what the rules governing the situation are.
2. They may believe that it is rude to go first and to put oneself in front of other people.

3. They may not like breaking silences.
4. They may not like being the centre of the whole group's attention.
5. They may feel it is embarrassing to break from the group (who are all silent and waiting) and strike out alone.

Embarrassment, or the threat of embarrassment, can have a particularly strong hold in children, where the influence of peer pressure tends to be at its greatest.

Aside from these reasons explaining why students might not want to speak, there are also reasons as to why students may feel they do not have anything to contribute.

First among these is the fact that, at the start of a discussion, nothing has been said. This means that there is no reference point against which to judge one's own ideas or from which to deduce criteria which indicate what sort of comments are expected. Accordingly, students may well anticipate (rightly or wrongly) that what they think about the topic or what they would like to say may not be of relevance or, even worse, may be inappropriate.

Second, students may lack confidence. This can lead them to be unfairly critical of their own ideas or arguments. Such a situation is compounded by the apparent confidence which most students perceive as being necessary if one is to start talking to the rest of the group in a silent room. Further, the lack of reference criteria noted in the last paragraph means there is no rejoinder to a student's unrealistic internal standards, the standards by which they are falsely judging their own thoughts to be unworthy of sharing.

A really successful method for overcoming all these difficulties is to avoid beginning any discussion in silence with the whole class sat waiting for someone to say something. Instead, pose the question, give the statement or indicate the topic and ask students to spend thirty to sixty seconds talking this over with their partners.

The room will immediately fill with noise. The barriers to speaking identified above simply do not apply in paired discussion. Once sufficient time has elapsed, get the class quiet again and ask a pair to share what they talked about, or ask one half of a pair to explain what the other half said. Repeat the process with another couple of pairs or use what was first said to spark up a discussion.

By talking with a partner first, students are able to check that their views are sound in an environment which feels safe. They are able to develop some reference points based on what their partner says. They are able to discuss without hesitation because they are face-to-face rather than individual-to-group. They are then able to talk to the whole group more easily because they do not have to report their own views if they do not wish (removing the fear of failure), they have already spent time discussing whatever is at issue, and the room has been filled with noise, dispelling that initial anxiety at breaking a silence.

The 'partners first' technique can be used throughout a discussion. It is not exclusively for the beginning. It is also a good way of ensuring everybody in the room gets a chance to speak about whatever is at issue and has their own ideas heard, something which will not always be possible in the traditional whole-class discussion format.

14. Stimulus Material

There are many different ways to begin a discussion in the classroom. The most common, and one which is continually referred to in this book, is to present students with a question or statement related to the topic of study. There is also the frequently used method of providing students with a task which they must fulfil, the results of which will form the basis of a discussion. In a formulation such as this, students are investigating a topic and subsequently talking about the results of that investigation.

Another way of starting discussion is through the use of stimulus material. Here, the teacher presents students with something and asks them to respond to it; the material is, literally, stimulating pupils into thinking.

It is an approach which is not appropriate in every setting. For example, if students already know a great deal about a topic and the teacher wishes them to use this knowledge in a discussion, then stimulus material will be a distraction rather than a help. Similarly, if students have completed a task, or a series of tasks, which were designed to lead up to a discussion, then any stimulus material is likely to get in the way of the lesson flow. It will detract from what has been planned, rather than add to it.

It is most effective to use stimulus material when any of the following apply:

1. Students have not done much, or any, prior work on the topic.
2. The teacher wants to focus on something specific which can be easily accessed through certain resources.
3. The purpose of the discussion is to 'get students thinking about a topic'.
4. The teacher wishes to challenge students' thinking (this can include encouraging students to think critically or creatively).
5. The material is being used as an introduction to a topic or to an idea; discussion will draw out existing knowledge and lead on to other tasks concerning the topic or idea.

The stimulus material for which a teacher opts can take many forms. It could be an image, a part of a text, a historical document, an object, a speech, a newspaper article, a photograph, an event or a piece of music. The list could go on; it is highly inclusive.

Once the material has been chosen, the teacher must decide how they will introduce it to students, how they will frame it and how they will use it to build a discussion. We will look at each of these points in turn.

Introducing the material, the teacher has three options: say nothing, say a little or say a lot. The first option has the advantage of not pre-empting student thoughts and of not priming pupils to look at the material in a certain way. The main drawback is that the ambiguity may be too great for some students, leading them to not engage with the activity and to make no response. The second option requires the teacher to consider what precisely they want pupils to know about the material. This judgement ought to take into account the underlying purpose of using the stimulus material. For example, if the purpose is to provoke a creative discussion, then it will be best not to reveal too many specific points about the material as these could stymie original thinking. The third option allows the teacher to contextualise the material for students and to scaffold possible responses which they might make when they interact with it. The disadvantage here is that the teacher may unwittingly close down avenues of thought or inadvertently direct students to specific ways of thinking, thus limiting the scope of the discussion which follows.

Having introduced the material, the teacher will need to frame it for students, telling them how they ought to interact with it. On a very basic level this could simply involve the teacher asking a question such as: 'What might this be?' or 'How might this connect to the subject?' A more detailed framing might involve a preamble in which the teacher picks out certain aspects of the material and intimates how they might be thought about or what questions might be asked of them. An extensive framing will see the teacher specifying precisely what it is students are expected to do with the material and, consequently, what they should have ready to contribute to the discussion. In this case, for example, the teacher may ask different pairs to analyse a specific line of text, making use of a set of questions to do so.

Once students have interacted with the stimulus material and thought about their responses it will be time for the discussion to begin. The teacher will need to judge whether the ensuing debate must remain close to the stimulus material, or whether it can just be used as a jumping-off point. Such a judgement will be dependent on the choice of stimulus material and its intended purpose, as well as the overarching aims on which the lesson as a whole is built. Here are two examples to demonstrate this point:

- **Example 1:** Stimulus material = Passage of dialogue from a Dickens novel. Students will be studying this novel over the next few months. This may lead the teacher to keep the discussion close to the material.
- **Example 2:** Stimulus material = A picture of an animal in a cage. Students will be studying the English legal system over the next three weeks. Here it will be best to use the stimulus material as a jumping-off point.

Stimulus material can provoke fantastic discussions in class. It can grab students' attention, get them thinking and cause them to engage with the subject and the lesson. By thinking about when and how to use it, the teacher is able to maximise these benefits and ensure that they are harnessed and not allowed to dissipate.

15. Identifying the Purpose of Discussion

It is important to identify the purpose behind a discussion as this allows the teacher to direct matters accordingly and to judge whether or not the activity has been successful. If one cannot accurately state why discussion is to be used, then it is up for debate whether sufficient thought has gone into the planning of the lesson.

It may be that a teacher uses a discussion activity without having clear reasons as to why they have opted for it and without any knowledge as to what specific purposes the discussion is meant to serve. Such a teacher may get lucky and be part of a brilliant, engaging lesson in which the use of discussion looks, to outsiders, like a masterstroke. If, however, that teacher cannot explain why they used discussion or what purposes it was intended to fulfil, then they are likely to repeat the feat only by chance. What is more, they will not be in possession of understanding. This means that they will not be a skilled user of discussion and will not be maximising their chances of continually using it successfully (I say 'maximising their chances' because there is always a possibility that a discussion may fall flat).

Identifying the purpose of a discussion need not be onerous. It can usually be done in under a minute. It requires the teacher to think about what they want the discussion to do in the context of the lesson and how it will help students to learn. Here are some examples of purposes of discussions:

- To allow students to hear different opinions and ideas about a topic
- To give students the opportunity to develop understanding by working with others
- To analyse a specific concept
- To interrogate a proposition
- To rehearse a range of arguments concerning a contention
- To give students the opportunity to develop their reasoning
- To help students actively engage with information they have previously studied
- To provide a space in which to develop ideas
- To allow the teacher to hear what students think (and to use this information to inform their teaching)
- To engage students in a specific topic

Some of these are quite general, some far more specific. In any one discussion it is likely that there will be a number of purposes, perhaps with one dominating and the rest being seen as important yet subordinate.

Having identified the purpose, or purposes, behind the use of discussion in a lesson, the teacher will be in a better position to decide what type of discussion to use (generic paired, group or whole-class or a specific discussion-based activity) and how this ought to be structured. There will be a clear driving force informing the planning of discussion which would otherwise have been absent. This will inevitably lead to better, more focussed planning and, as a result, better learning and greater student progress.

The only risk is that, having identified a purpose, the teacher may be tempted to over-elaborate in their planning due to a desire to ensure the wished-for outcomes are achieved. This is a potential pitfall common to all planning. The best advice is to not do it; too much planning will obscure interactions between students and between teacher and students. It will also result in a lack of flexibility and is likely to draw the teacher's attention away from what is happening in the classroom – both in terms of behaviour and in terms of intellectual endeavour – because they will be focussed on their plan and its implementation.

In many situations it can be beneficial to share the purpose of a discussion with your students. Doing so provides clarity and gives a greater sense of meaning to the activity. It will also help pupils to assess their own contributions and those made by their peers. In addition, the teacher can use the purpose they have disclosed as a means to draw students back should they veer off topic or become disengaged. Pupils will understand the language and are likely to acknowledge its relevance because of the time already taken by the teacher to speak about it.

Sharing the purpose of a discussion requires a brief consideration of what language will be most appropriate. Depending on the age of your class, you may need to couch your explanation in terms quite different from those that you would use with a colleague. While this is an obvious point, it is one worth making. It is better to cover the step prior to beginning the lesson. Making a quick conversion from professional- to student-language while pupils are sat staring up at you is not always as easy as one might assume. Doing the work beforehand – and it does not take long – is generally a good idea.

There will be times, of course, when it will be best not to share the purpose of a discussion or, at the very least, to share only some of the purposes. For example, if you intend to use the discussion as an aid to assessment then divulging this to students may cause them to clam up or to act in a manner which is contrary to what is usually the case. Equally, if the purpose of a discussion is to encourage students to think creatively about a topic then it might be better just to get on with it; sometimes, being told that one is expected to be creative can prove a significant hindrance to original thinking.

16. Choosing the Level of Control

It is for the teacher to decide how much control they wish to exert over a discussion. This control can be in relation to what is discussed, how it is discussed, when it is discussed and by whom it is discussed. We will look at each of these points in turn.

What Is to Be Discussed?

In many cases the teacher will decide what is to be discussed, basing their choice on the lesson topic. In their planning they will identify a particular area of the topic which is conducive to discussion and will arrange an appropriate activity accordingly. This will involve choosing stimulus material, a pre-discussion task or a question or statement which students will be expected to debate about. There are thus two choices: (i) The topic which is to be discussed and (ii) The specific part of that topic on which focus is to fall.

There is an alternative approach. It can be richly rewarding, on occasion, to leave it to pupils to decide what is to be discussed. The risk is that those areas the teacher believes are important may be completely ignored. The great benefits are that students will choose what they believe to be important or interesting and are likely to be highly motivated as a result.

It is best to use some kind of structure through which to elicit student suggestions. This can be an extended, formal process such as in the Philosophy for Children model (see chapter 3) or a short one such as asking students to think of ideas based around a couple of generic question cues (What do you think is interesting about this topic? What area of this topic should we talk more about?). It is generally a good thing to ask students to vote on a range of options which the class have come up with. If you decide on one of the suggestions yourself then the reasons for having student-led discussion in the first place are somewhat lost.

How Is It to Be Discussed?

We will delineate the various levels of control one many choose:

- **High level of control:** You have specific aims for the discussion and are prepared to subjugate all else to achieve these. As such, you have planned in advance the timings and how the activity is to run. You may have prepared a list of questions which you want all students to have discussed by the end of the allotted time. There may also be certain teaching points you wish to make and which you plan to draw out whether or not an opportunity arises.
- **Medium level of control:** You have aims for the discussion but believe these can be achieved through a variety of means. You have planned some timings but remain flexible; you judge that students may wish to explore more than what you have presupposed. You will have some prompts ready to guide the discussion toward certain areas although you are happy for students to make their own way once you have set them going in a general direction.
- **Low level of control:** You have broad aims for the discussion. You trust your students and believe they are capable of discussing with care and skill despite not having a tight structure in which to work. You act as a facilitator and let students lead the way. You may invite one or more students to head up the discussion or allow the class, groups or pairs to police themselves.

When Is It to Be Discussed?

There is not a great deal to be said for this category. Generally the teacher will expect all class members to be engaged in discussion at the same time, whether that discussion is in pairs, groups or as a whole class. On occasion, students may be asked to work through a range of activities or tasks independent of the teacher, in groups or in pairs. In such cases it will be up to the students to decide in what order they approach their work. If discussion is included on the list of things to do, pupils will choose when to do it. In general though, the teacher will maintain tight control over when discussion takes place.

Who Is to Discuss It?

The choice here revolves around whether you want paired, group or whole-class discussion. The latter is likely to involve the greatest level of control as, in the majority of cases, it will be the teacher who indicates who is to speak next. This will be true even when there are a series of student-student interactions because, if not, there is the risk that the discussion will descend into a clamour of competing voices, each wishing desperately to be heard. The teacher does not have to interject their own voice in order to move from one speaker to the next; it can be done non-verbally with the outstretching of a palm or the nod of a head.

Paired discussion means the teacher still exerts a reasonably strong level of control. This is because each pair will be obliged to speak to one another, with it being difficult for any individual to avoid taking part. If they do, then their partner will be prevented from engaging in discussion. Such a situation will be easy for the teacher to spot; intervention can follow to redirect the disengaged student back onto task. A pitfall which is harder to identify involves two students giving the appearance of completing the task when, in actual fact, they are speaking about something other than the work. The best way to avoid this happening is through judicious pairings in which those liable to go off topic and those who are close friends are kept apart.

Group discussion sees the teacher ceding far more control than in the previous two cases. Even if groups are kept to reasonable sizes (three is recommended, four at a push) so as to ensure there is an onus on all members to participate, the risk remains that some students will 'sit it out', leaving others to do the work. Further, because there is an expectation that not everyone in a group will be talking at the same time, it is harder to pick out pupils who are not engaging with the task. The teacher will have to be more vigilant if they are to ensure that everyone is working; they may have to accept that it will be impossible for them to be certain. If that is the case then the question becomes one of costs and benefits: Do the benefits of group discussion with this class outweigh the potential costs? If the answer is 'yes' then the ceding of control can be happily accepted. If the answer is 'no' then alternative activities need to be found.

17. Philosophical Discussions

Philosophy is a difficult subject to define. Its nature has changed over time. Things which were previously central to it are now recognised as disciplines of their own (for example, the natural sciences). Further, the various branches of philosophy which exist today are not uniformly accepted as belonging to the discipline. On the other hand, what remains common throughout philosophical investigations is the application of reasoning to matters of deep importance which do not appear to be amenable to empirical analysis. In a sense, philosophy's subject matter is thought: its nature, structure and the claims which are made from and within it. Five key areas form the central locus of study; the ascription of these to the remit of philosophy is uncontroversial. They are: logic, ethics, metaphysics, aesthetics, and epistemology. Much modern British philosophy has also concerned itself with the nature and meaning of language.

The beauty of philosophy, for me anyway, is that it reaches out towards that which is most fundamental in our thinking and challenges us to look at it critically and fearlessly. It is for this reason that I would suggest it should be used in discussions. Encouraging students to think philosophically will help them to think more clearly about themselves and the world. It will also help them to think with greater care and logic about other areas of thought.

In any discussion there will be opportunities to turn the debate toward philosophical investigation. Three areas in particular tend to be touched on again and again, each of which is outlined below. Upon familiarising yourself with these areas you will be in a position to identify when they come up and to decide whether or not the time is ripe for a philosophical detour.

Concepts

Concepts are those things which are thought or imagined. Nearly always they will refer to something which is perceived to be in the world but which does not have a tangible existence. Courage is a concept. Clearly there are examples of courage in the world. We probably all know, or have at least heard of, people who we would consider to have behaved courageously. Yet, if we were asked to go out and find courage, we would not be able to do so. We might be able to find a person who could be said to have courage, or who could be said to have acted courageously, but surely we could not say that we had found courage? The most we could say is that we have found a person who is said to have courage or has shown courage by acting courageously. This would not mean that we had courage itself, though, only examples of it. Concepts such as courage are mental formations which we apply to the world but which do not exist independently in the world.

When we communicate we rely heavily on concepts. They form the bedrock of our language and are used by all of us in nearly all of our speech and writing. One area of philosophical investigation which can be drawn into classroom discussions is the analysis of concepts. This involves fixing on a concept which is being used in the discussion and spending time investigating its meaning and the way in which it is used in different settings. Here is an example:

In a Geography lesson about tourism the class may be discussing the question: On balance, is tourism of benefit to the local population? Such a discussion is likely to include various arguments for and against the proposition 'tourism benefits locals'. Turning the discussion toward philosophical analysis might involve asking students to spend some time thinking about the meaning and use of the word 'benefit'. What actually is a benefit? How does your standpoint affect the way in which you judge if something is beneficial or not? In what sense are we using the word 'benefit' (in the sense of an advantage, something which helps or a subsidy)? Such a sub-discussion is both an end in itself and also a benefit(!) to the wider discussion, providing as it does greater clarity regarding one of the lesson's key terms.

Ethics

The concerns of ethics (or moral philosophy) cover three distinct yet related areas:

- Questions of right and wrong

- Questions concerning how what is deemed to be right and what is deemed to be wrong is so defined and how one can make, or ought to go about making, moral judgements
- The application of moral reasoning to specific situations

Many classroom discussions present opportunities to investigate the ethical positions students hold. Any judgement which asserts that something is either right or wrong is an ethical judgement. Such judgements as these will rest on some set of criteria, usually linked to a hierarchy of values. They will not necessarily be logically consistent.

Ethical discussions should focus on the reasons students give for the ethical positions they advocate. The purpose is to encourage pupils to think critically about their own values and why it is that they suppose them to be right, particularly if other students are promoting a different position. There may be times when such analysis leads a student to alter their own views. This is not the end goal of ethical discussion but a supplement which may or may not come about. The overarching intention, which should be pursued throughout, is to make students think rationally about their own moral positions. In some cases this will result in them re-asserting their original views with stronger reasoning than was originally the case; at other times it may cause them to change their views; another possibility still is that, in spite of any doubt cast by discussion, they retain their views, discarding argument in favour of intuition.

Here are three means through which you can challenge students' ethical thinking:

1. **Ask for reasoning.** Many ethical positions are asserted without any reasoning to back them up. Asking students for reasons will cause them to think in more detail about why they hold certain views. Be sure to press reasoning – a common attempt at escape sees students falling back on circular reasoning (which is sometimes legitimate but generally not).

2. **Use thought experiments.** This involves imagining a situation and asking students to apply their ethical positions to it. The purpose is to test whether or not the judgements will hold. In so doing, one is assessing the logic which underpins them, the scope of application which they possess and the hierarchy of values on which they depend. For example, a student asserts that

it is wrong to eat animals. A thought experiment could be: 'You are on a desert island and there is no food. Do you try to catch and eat fish from the sea?'

3. **Suggest alternative viewpoints.** When students put forward ethical positions, ask them to reimagine the situation from another perspective. This will encourage them to think about their own judgements from a point of view other than their own. For example, a student asserts that positive discrimination is fundamentally unjust. An alternative standpoint might be that of someone who has continually been passed over for promotion, seemingly for discriminatory reasons. Asking the same student to think about their assertion from this position will be taxing but rewarding.

Epistemology

Epistemology is that branch of philosophy which deals with issues of knowledge. It is informed by questions such as 'What can we know?' 'How certain can we be about the knowledge we think we have about the world?' 'Is it possible to have objective knowledge or is all knowledge bound by subjective experience?' Clearly, some of these questions will not be appropriate for discussions focussed on some other matter; they are perhaps too overwhelming to work as a supplement.

It can be helpful to detour into epistemological territory that is a touch lighter and which impacts on the main discussion in important ways but not to such an extent that it overpowers the point which is at issue. Students will often make comments or put forward arguments which contain potential problems regarding the knowledge they claim to rely on, or the way(s) of knowing about the world they have used to derive this knowledge. It may also be the case that what is being discussed is itself requiring of epistemological analysis.

Here are some questions which may prove fruitful in getting students to think about the status of knowledge:

- How can you know that? This could be asked in many situations, not least when a student has put forward an opinion which appears to rest on flimsy foundations.

- ◆ How can you be certain that what you say is true? This question is particularly useful for getting students to look at the nature of certainty and what the implications might be for their own knowledge of the world.

- ◆ How can we know that something is true? This is a good question to use if the concept of truth has already arisen in the discussion. It invites a deeper exploration of that idea.

- ◆ How do we acquire knowledge? This question will cause students to think about how they can come to be able to make assertions or arguments and whether they are in fact justified in doing so.

- ◆ What does X refer to and is it something of which we can have knowledge? In this question, X will usually be a concept which is central to the issue being discussed. Analysing the epistemological status of that concept ought to improve the quality of the debate and identify what can and cannot be known with regard to it.

18. Non-Verbal Discussion

The dominant view of discussion is talking of some kind between two or more people, usually with the intention of sharing ideas, debating an issue or as an attempt to reach some sort of conclusion. A discussion does not by necessity have to conform to this definition; it could involve a written exchange between two or more people. In this sense, it is perhaps useful to think of discussion as a dialogue; a back-and-forth exchange of ideas or opinions which can be conducted through writing as well as through speech.

In the classroom, one of the key reasons for using discussion is the benefits for learning which come from being able to talk about one's own ideas and from being able to listen to other people talk about their ideas. Speech is functionally and structurally different to writing; incorporating it in the classroom allows one to take advantage of this fact. There may be times though when the opportunity for non-verbal discussion presents itself and the teacher decides that further benefits can be obtained by following this up. Here are some examples of non-verbal discussions in society at large:

- Newspaper letters pages
- Internet forums
- Internet sites where comments can be posted (for example, after a feature article)
- Judicial decisions which include dissenting opinions
- Letters written between people
- Email exchanges
- Written negotiations (usually between parties who are not prepared to speak to one another)
- Text messages in which some issue is debated

Not all of these can be transposed to the classroom. Here are five alternatives which take account of the practicalities of working in school:

- **Post-it® Note Dialogues:** Students are presented with a series of questions which are displayed or written on the board. They are given a collection of blank Post-it® notes and tasked with writing a response to each of the questions. When they have done this, they stick each note on the board beside the question to which it is a response. Next, students read the answers other pupils have posted. They then comment on these by writing out a new Post-it® note and sticking this onto the answer to which they are responding. The process is repeated until pupils have used up all of their Post-it® notes.

- **Silent Debate:** This is explained in more detail in chapter 3. Briefly, it consists of the following: A number of large sheets of paper are distributed around the room. Each of these has a question or statement written on it. Students walk around the room, in silence, with a pen in hand. They are tasked with writing a comment on each of the pieces of paper which responds to the question or statement. Following this, they continue to walk around the room except now they read the comments their peers have written. They comment on these comments, creating a debate between different members of the class in purely written form.

- **Intranet Forums:** An intranet is an internal network; it cannot be accessed by anyone who is not on a school computer. It is thus safer for use with students than the internet, which is a public domain. If you have the appropriate technology available (for example, a managed learning environment) then you can set up a forum in which students debate an issue between themselves. The discussion could take place during a lesson if computer facilities are available. Alternatively, the forum could be set up by the teacher and pupils could be asked to make a contribution for homework. The teacher could start the next lesson by bringing up the forum on the interactive whiteboard or creating a hand-out of some of the most interesting comments, following this up with verbal discussion and analysis.

- **Comment-Only Marking:** This involves the teacher marking a student's work and providing them with feedback through the use of a written comment. This might be in the form of three strengths and one target. To turn this into a non-verbal discussion, the teacher should give students time to respond to the comments. The response should be written in their books, underneath the teacher's feedback. The teacher can then continue the discussion the next time the books are marked.

  In order to make the most of this method, it is preferable to have a comments sheet at the front of the book. Teacher comments and student responses can be recorded on this, creating an on-going dialogue. By collating all the feedback at the front of the book, it avoids the difficulty of having to move back and forth through the pages in search of the last comments which were made.

- **Letter Writing:** Non-verbal discussion of this type sees students reaching out of the classroom into the wider world. Set up a task which involves writing a letter to someone who holds a position in society relevant to the topic you are currently studying. Here are some examples:
  - Topic = Poetry. Position in society = Poet; Rapper; Classical Actor.
  - Topic = Earthquakes. Position in society = Geologist; Seismologist; Someone working in disaster relief.
  - Topic = Christianity. Position in society = Priest; Bishop; Archbishop.

All the letters from a class could be sent off, a selection, a single 'winning entry' or a composite. Whichever is the case, questions ought to be included in the letters so that the recipient has something which they can answer, in order to form a dialogue. Upon receiving a response, and if it is appropriate, a follow-up letter could be sent, extending the discussion.

It may be best to contact the person to whom you are asking students to write before sending the letters off. This way you can check to see if they are both willing and able to respond. If necessary, the teacher can contact a number of people in advance and divide their class up so that different groups of students are tasked with writing letters to the different contacts the teacher has sounded out.

An excellent wall display can be created out of the letters sent by students and the responses they receive.

19. Capturing Progress

It is a commonly held criticism of discussion that, as a teaching device, it lacks the all-important ability to capture progress. Someone coming into a classroom in which discussion has been used, it is argued, will be unable to tell from looking at student books what progress has been made. Therefore, whatever benefits there might be in using discussion are negated by the fact that little or no record of student work will exist. Two inferences are often drawn from this: (i) because there is nothing to show, discussion itself is not work and (ii) because there is no means by which to check what students have done, they can easily avoid doing any work if they so wish. There are a number of ways in which the progress made in a discussion can be captured and we will look at these below. Before we do, however, it is worth unpacking some of the assumptions in the anti-discussion view we have outlined above.

What constitutes progress? Learning, certainly, but how does this manifest itself? One would think it would generally be in the form of increased knowledge of some particular subject or a better understanding of that subject. That these two things intertwine goes without saying.

Capturing progress is a different matter from trying to define what it is. The notion is predicated on the idea that progress *can* be captured and that it *ought* to be captured. The language stems from the assessment of teachers through statutory and in-school frameworks. The driving purpose is to make judgements about effectiveness. In order to make a judgement, one needs criteria. In an administrative sense, particularly one that is top-down and hierarchical, specific measures are preferable as they give the suggestion of uniformity across a large sample. This means that two types of judgement can be made:

1. Judgements of individuals in relation to a set of criteria.
2. Judgements of how individual judgements compare across various levels (local, regional, national, international).

A system or framework which is based on this will not welcome the lack of concrete data which discussion provides; unless the assessor sits through the discussions teacher and students engage in, there is nothing they can use as the basis for their judgements.

The assumption that because there is nothing to show therefore discussion does not involve any work is lazy. All of us have engaged in strenuous thinking with seemingly nothing to show for it. Consider:

- Wrestling with a major life decision such as whether to relocate, have another child or file for a divorce.
- Analysing a new situation in detail before deciding how to act.
- Coming up with sound responses under pressure in an interview for a new job.

In each of these cases no tangible product is created. The first results in changed circumstances but the thinking behind these would only become known if the individual chose to reveal it. Many people would look at the situation from the outside and simply assume a decision had been made and no more.

The fact is that many of the things we do in our lives are not recorded or made evident, yet they are still premised on thinking which is in-depth and often difficult. The contrast with writing – which forms a large part of the work done in the classroom – is detrimental to one's view of such actions. Writing is fixed by nature – that is one of the major benefits it provides to mankind (it coheres over time; once it is recorded it remains as it is). Therefore, any task which involves writing will logically include a tangible product; unless the student chooses not to write, nothing else can be the case. In a sense then, writing can come to be placed at the top of a hierarchy, its position given due to the fact that it can speak for itself across space and time (something which many other actions or means of communicating cannot do).

If a discussion creates no product, then some assume that students will be able to choose not to do anything and that they will get away with this. Such an argument is not exclusive to discussion activities. Students have the means to avoid doing work no matter what the activity is; they can put down tools surreptitiously or with great ostentation and then refuse to work at any point in any lesson. There is only so much the teacher can do.

Invariably, however, this is not the case. Most students tend to do what is asked of them and the teacher has various means at their disposal by which to encourage or compel recalcitrant learners back on track. In a high-quality discussion there will always be something for every student to be doing: listening, speaking, thinking and making notes are some of the commonest examples. This means that if any student does try to avoid doing work, the teacher will know that this is the case. In addition, the use of the various activity structures and techniques outlined in this book will help any teacher to ensure that all their pupils are learning for the entirety of a discussion.

All this said, we must strive to avoid an either/or situation in which discussion is set against other forms of classroom activity. Capturing progress can be a useful part of any discussion. Moulded to complement the main task, rather than tacked on as an added extra, it can help students and teacher to get more out of a debate. The teacher will always need to exercise their professional judgement in order to assess whether, during the course of a discussion, it will be useful to capture progress made by learners or whether it may prove a hindrance.

Here are a variety of ways to capture progress:

- ◆ Precede discussion with a written activity as outlined earlier in this section. Follow the discussion with an assessment or redrafting of the written work.
- ◆ Follow a discussion activity with a written task as outlined earlier in this section. In such cases, the content and quality of the writing will be a direct consequence of the thinking and learning which has taken place during the discussion.
- ◆ Include some sort of written element in the discussion activity. In the next chapter, examples are given of how this might be done. In general, it could be in the form of note-taking, one

person taking on the role of 'scribe' or a switch during the activity from talking to writing ('OK, take two minutes to write down your thoughts on what we have heard so far').

- Assign roles to students in paired, group or whole-class discussions. These roles should be based on that pupil capturing the progress which is made. The role of 'scribe' has already been mentioned. Other roles include 'summariser' (who writes a summary of the key learning points at the end of a discussion), 'learning observer' (who writes during the discussion, but only writes what they think is new learning demonstrated by the group) and 'assessor' (who is given a sheet they have to fill in, assessing the discussion as it goes along and giving examples for each judgement they make).
- Record the discussion using a video camera or a microphone.
- At the end of a discussion, ask students to assess the discussion as a whole, the contribution which they made or the learning they feel they have got from the debate. Assessments could be made in workbooks or through using a pro-forma.

20. Using What Students Say

One of the assessments a teacher has to make during any discussion activity is when to intervene and, particularly, when to do things with what students say. At times it will be preferable to leave student comments as they are and to indicate who is to speak next. In such cases it is likely that the pupil whose turn it is will make some reference to what has just been said, even if this is only cursory.

At other times, the teacher will see an opportunity to use what a student has said in order to further the group's learning, to improve the quality of the discussion or to alter it altogether. Six methods which may be employed to achieve these various aims are outlined below (other approaches are scattered throughout this book):

- **Recasting:** This involves the teacher taking what the student has said and altering it while retaining the meaning. For example:

Student: Earthquakes are bad 'cos they smash up all the businesses and make a mess of people's homes

Teacher: That's right; earthquakes do have significant consequences, including damage to businesses and homes. What other consequences might earthquakes have?

The purpose of recasting is to acknowledge and praise correct answers given by students while also modelling the accurate and appropriate use of language. It is important to avoid sounding patronising when doing so. Also, the teacher does not necessarily need to draw attention to it; the frequent modelling of accurate and appropriate language through recasting should be sufficient in itself to raise the quality of a discussion.

- **Following-on:** This method sees the teacher being more 'hands-on' in the discussion. They do this in order to ensure that the points which are being made are duly regarded by other students. One common pitfall sees pupils making a series of unconnected comments; each contributor states what they think about the topic instead of engaging with what has already been said. The intellectual ramifications of this are clear – active thinking is not happening. Following-on involves the teacher taking what a student has said and asking other pupils to respond to it directly. It works like this:

Student: Henry VIII wasn't that bad – he was a victim of the time in which he lived.

Teacher: Thank you for the comment. Chris, what do you think about this? Was Henry a victim of the time in which he lived?

Another approach would be:

Student: Henry VIII wasn't that bad – he was a victim of the time in which he lived.

Teacher: OK, thirty seconds with your partner to discuss the idea – was Henry a victim of the time in which he lived?

- **Interrogating:** Opportunities will arise where it is preferable for the teacher to intervene in order to interrogate what a student has said rather than let it pass without comment. Such situations may include:
  - An assertion unsupported by reasons, evidence or examples.

- A comment which is ambiguous or difficult to comprehend.
- A comment which contains one or more assumptions.
- A comment which has interesting, unusual or far-reaching implications which have not been considered by the contributor.
- A comment which suggests prejudice or a discriminatory attitude.

In the first four cases the purpose of interrogation is to develop what has been said and, by extension, to improve the quality of the discussion. The teacher may ask questions of clarification, questions requesting further explanation or questions asking how counter-arguments or counter-examples may be satisfactorily dealt with. In the fifth case the issue is one of moral analysis. Such comments ought not to be left by the teacher. They should interrogate the reasoning behind these and, if this is not sufficient to dissuade the student, point out that the making of such comments is precluded in the context of a classroom debate.

- **Exemplifying:** Students make many excellent contributions to paired, group or whole-class discussions. The teacher can use these as examples or models of good practice. The process involves identifying a student comment which exemplifies something which is good, explaining to the rest of the class how and why it is good and praising the original student for making such a contribution. Here is an example:

Student: Young people do not have much of a chance to speak in the media. For example, nearly all the people who write for newspapers are adults. That means it is hard for teenagers to combat bad stereotypes.

Teacher: What an excellent comment. You have given an example which supports your case, showing how your argument plays out in today's world. As well as that, you have explained what the consequences are for teenagers. This makes it clear why your example is relevant to your initial point. Well done; a great contribution.

- **Supplementing:** On occasion, it may be that a student makes a comment which lends itself to being supplemented by the teacher. This will involve the teacher saying something more about the contribution in order to further the discussion. It may be that the teacher observes something intrinsic to the comment which it would be difficult for students to pick up on. Alternatively, the comment may give the teacher the opportunity to introduce some extra information or ideas of which the class may not be aware. One has to tread a fine line when it comes to supplementing. It must not be done too often as, even with the best will in the world, this will stymie the discussion, causing it to be weighted too heavily in favour of the teacher's voice. The key is to try and identify those times when supplementing what a student has said will be of greatest benefit to the class and to the continuing success of the discussion. As ever, it is a professional judgement – and one which may, at first, take a little time to refine.

- **Redirecting:** This method is simple. There are times when a discussion loses focus, goes round in circles, gets stuck on a tangential point or simply stops being of benefit (in terms of thinking and learning) to the participants. Should one of these situations arise, the teacher can use what a student says in order to redirect the discussion onto more fertile ground. This can be done in two ways:
    1. Identify something within a comment made by a student and use this as the basis of a new question for the group to discuss.
    2. Thank the student who has made the latest comment and then indicate that it draws that particular section of the discussion to a close. If necessary, explain how the topic has been exhausted or how the comments have lost focus (for whatever reason). Pose a new question or introduce a different topic and ask students to take up the discussion from there.

That brings our section on strategies and techniques to a close. We will now go on to look at a range of discussion activities, all of which are generic and appropriate for use with different topics and age groups.

CHAPTER THREE

Twenty Activities

In this chapter we look at twenty different activities which can be used to structure discussion. Each one is explained, exemplified, and supplemented by extensions and developments.

All the activities are practical, effective and ready to use. They can be tailored to work with nearly all areas of the curriculum and most age groups.

1. Circle Time

Explanation

Arrange the room so all the tables are moved to one side and the chairs are set out in a circle. Students and teacher take a seat, as well as any support staff who are working with the class. Sitting in a circle creates a sense of equality; no one is at the head or the front; each person has an equal position. For this reason, all those who are in the room should be included in the circle.

Explain to students that there will be a discussion in which everyone will have an opportunity to share their views, with no one being excluded. You should provide some sort of item which indicates whose turn it is to speak. This could be a soft toy, a foam ball or a conch shell, for example. The item is passed to the person who is to speak and they hold it while they are talking. Initially, the teacher decides who is to receive the item each time. As students become familiar with the activity they should be able to manage the turn-taking themselves.

The discussion starts off with the teacher providing a question, statement or some stimulus material. Students are asked to think about this, then to share their ideas with the person next to them. From this, a whole-group discussion ensues, with ideas and opinions flowing back and forth across the circle.

Example

Topic: Animal rights

The teacher begins by asking the class to rearrange the room into a circle of chairs. This allows students to immediately work in concert with one another, as will be the expectation when they engage in discussion. With pupils sat down, the teacher might choose to do a warm-up activity. Memory, drama and movement games tend to work best. There are three key reasons for doing such an activity. First, it breaks the ice and allows students time to familiarise themselves with the circle format. Second, it reinforces the sense of togetherness and of working as a group. Third, it allows the teacher to discreetly mix the pupils up (often students will sit in friendship or gender groups. This can hinder discussion).

The question 'Do animals have rights?' is placed on the board. Students are invited to think silently about this for thirty seconds or so. They are then asked to spend about a minute discussing their thoughts with the person sat next to them. Finally, the teacher draws the group back together and asks for a volunteer to begin the main discussion. They are given the speaker's item and the rest flows from there.

Extensions and Developments

1. Appoint one or two students to be in charge of the speaker's item. They decide who is to speak next (although this must be done fairly) and move the item from the current speaker to the next person.
2. Split the circle in two and ask each half to look at a different aspect of the question. In the above case this could be: (i) the nature of rights and (ii) the relationship between animals and humans. Bring the class back together and ask each side to share their findings.

2. Community of Enquiry

Explanation

A community of enquiry is a democratic way of developing discussion. Due to how it works, it tends to increase student motivation.

The room should be arranged as per Circle Time, that is, in a circle of chairs with any tables pushed to one side. Students, teacher and any support staff sit in the circle and a warm-up activity is used if the teacher feels it is appropriate (that which is explained in the entry on Circle Time applies here as well).

The teacher then explains that the discussion will focus on a question or statement created by members of the group and chosen through a class vote. One of two paths can be followed here. Either the teacher indicates the topic which questions or statements should be based on, or they present some stimulus material and invite students to develop from this whatever questions they would like to discuss.

Students work in groups of three to five (depending on the class size) to produce their questions or statements. When everyone is ready, each group in turn reads out what they have come up with, providing a supplementary explanation if necessary. Having heard all of the options the class votes; the most popular question or statement forms the basis of the discussion.

This method is similar to that of Philosophy for Children (see www.sapere.org.uk for more information). It is advisable to encourage students to aim for conceptual questions rather than concrete ones, as these provide greater scope for discussion.

Example

Topic: Designing products which benefit consumers

Students rearrange the room into a circle of chairs. The teacher explains the topic and indicates that the questions or statements groups produce should directly relate to it. The class is divided into groups of three or four and each one is given some paper and a pen. Students then have five minutes in which to discuss their ideas before settling on a question or statement they feel happy putting forward to the whole class.

Each question or statement is heard in turn, with a volunteer scribing these on the board for everyone to see. Voting can take place in a number of ways: students close their eyes and put their hands up as the teacher reads out their favoured choice; by secret ballot; or through preferential voting, whereby each student can vote for a first, second and third choice (with three votes going to the first, two to the second and one to the third). The board is wiped and the winning question or statement is written up again, this time larger and in the centre. Discussion ensues, starting with contributions from the group whose question it was. An example question for this topic might be: 'What is a benefit?' or, 'How do you know something is a benefit to consumers?'

Extensions and Developments

1. Give each group the opportunity to advocate for their question. They should have a specific length of time (to make it fair) and must refrain from making negative comments about any other questions or statements.
2. If a number of questions prove popular, save the ones which just missed out on being discussed and follow up on these in future lessons.

3. Rainbow Groups

Explanation

This activity generates two discussions. In the first, a series of different groups discuss different topics. In the second, the members of those groups disband and then re-form in new groupings so as to share the results of all of the first discussions. It works as follows:

Begin by dividing the class into groups of five. Provide each group with a different topic or question which they are to discuss. This might be supplemented by some resources which the students are to investigate (with the results forming the basis of their discussions). How long is sufficient for this part of the activity will vary according to the ability levels in your class and the topic under consideration. Ten to fifteen minutes is usually about right. There may need to be some structure or direction to help students maintain their discussions. This could be in the form of a set of questions to work through or a pro-forma which needs to be filled in.

Next, take enough colours to cover each member of each group. So, if we have groups containing five students, red, green, orange, yellow and blue will be enough. Assign each group member a different colour. Ask the groups to disband. Explain that the new groups will be formed by the colours banding together. All the students who were assigned 'red' will form a new group, as will all the students who were assigned 'green' and so on.

Each member of the new colour-coded groups takes it in turn to relay what was discussed in their original group. These reports are discussed in turn. At the conclusion of the final report and discussion, the group reflects on all that has been said and looks for connections and differences between the various ideas and arguments which have been shared.

Example

Topic: The Great Depression

There are twenty-five students. As such, the teacher divides the class into five groups, each containing five students. The areas for discussion are distributed as follows:

Group One: How influential was the stock market crash of 1929?

Group Two: Were the banks to blame?

Group Three: What role was played by consumer spending?

Group Four: Was the Great Depression hastened by America's protectionist policies?

Group Five: Would things have been the same if there had not been a drought in 1930?

Each group spends ten to fifteen minutes discussing their question. In this example, the class have already spent time studying the main topic. The activity is being used to apply prior knowledge, to compare different perspectives and to analyse and evaluate various arguments.

Once the time is up, the members of each group have a colour assigned to them. These could be the same colours as those used above: red, green, orange, yellow and blue. The new, colour-coded groups come together. Each has a representative of one of the five earlier discussions. Therefore, each new group gets the opportunity to hear a synthesised account of the points made in the first part of the activity. Further discussion ensues in which students are able to draw together the various elements of the whole topic.

Extensions and Developments

1. Used in the manner outlined above, in the example, this activity is excellent preparation for a piece of extended writing. It gives students the chance to rehearse a range of arguments, to hear the results of investigations into a range of areas, and to make connections between different elements of a topic.
2. In the first part of the activity, assign the role of scribe to one member of each group. This person should make detailed notes on what is discussed. The teacher can then collect these in and photocopy them, creating a booklet for all the students in the class.

4. Snowballing

Explanation

Imagine a snowball rolling down a snow-covered hill. The more it travels the more mass it picks up. As it progresses, the snow which is in its path is removed from the ground and becomes part of the snowball. At the bottom of the hill it stops rolling. It is considerably larger than what it was at the start of its journey. This activity works on a similar principle: the movement from small to large through the accumulation of similar material.

To begin, students are asked to think silently about a question, statement or topic. They are invited to make a few notes about their thoughts. They are then are asked to turn to the person next to them and to share what they have come up with. The newly formed pairs discuss their ideas and compare notes. They search for common ground and identify on what points they are in agreement. Pairs are then asked to form a group of four with another pair. The process of sharing is repeated, with each pair taking it in turns to relay their thoughts and notes, including an explanation of those points on which they reached agreement and those points which remained contentious.

Finally, everyone is brought back together by the teacher and different groups of four share their thoughts with the whole class. The comments which are made here can form the basis of a whole-class discussion or can be left unchallenged (the choice should be predicated on what the teacher has decided is the purpose of the discussion).

Example

Topic: Imagery in a poem

The activity begins with each student thinking about how imagery is used in a poem which the class have recently been studying. Pupils note down their thoughts; these might include specific examples from the text, general comments, arguments or queries.

The teacher signals for students to move into pairs. Each pair discusses their ideas. It may be, for example, that in one pair, Student A feels the use of imagery is derivative and lacking in originality whereas Student B feels it is designed to conform to a particular tradition. Such a disagreement would lead to a useful discussion. The students would also be able to identify that they are in agreement about what the imagery is and where it is used in the poem; their dispute rests on the analysis of that imagery, not its existence or location.

The discussion snowballs again as pairs move into groups of four. In our example it may be that Student A is now outnumbered three to one and has to argue persuasively for their point of view in order to be heard by the group. Finally, the whole-class discussion may uncover a similar dissenting theme across the class. This could then being discussed and come to form the basis of a subsequent piece of written work.

Extensions and Developments

1. When students are thinking individually, ask them to note down three points. They should share these in their pairs and whittle down the six points they have to three points on which they agree. In groups of four, these three points are shared and the resulting six points are whittled back down; the group of four must agree on the three key points which they wish to take forward to the whole-class discussion.

2. An alternative method is to go from thinking individually to working in a group of three to working in a group of six. This is harder to manage (particularly the groups of six) but presents students with a different discussion experience.

5. Card Talk

Explanation

This activity uses cards to encourage students to discuss a range of different aspects of a topic. It is appropriate for use with pairs or groups. If you go for the latter, three or four is the ideal number per group.

Create a set of cards, each of which contains a key word, phrase, question or statement related to the topic you are studying. Having done this, photocopy the cards so that you have sufficient sets for the number of students in your class (you will need to think at this point about whether they will be working in pairs or groups).

Begin the activity in the lesson by moving students into pairs or groups. Give each pair or group a set of cards. The cards should be given out face down, so that what is written on them cannot be seen. Charge one member of each pair or group with stewardship of the cards.

Explain to the class what is on the cards and that, on the teacher's say so, the stewards should turn over the top card (or select one at random from the pack) and the pairs or group should start discussing whatever is written on that particular card. At timed intervals the teacher will signal for a new card to be drawn; the discussion will then move on to whatever topic is written on that card.

An alternative method, which is easier on the resources, involves the teacher making one set of cards and asking a member of the class to choose a card at random. The teacher then calls out what is written on the card and the pairs or groups begin their discussions. This is repeated as many times as the teacher sees fit.

Example

Topic: Human biology

Examples of what might be written on the cards:

- The various words and phrases: circulatory system; respiratory system; haemoglobin; hormone; organ
- The various questions: What role has natural selection played in the development of the human body? How do muscles function? Is there an ideal diet? What might be the consequences of being vaccinated?
- The various statements: Explanations in biology rely on chemistry and physics; Genes are the key influence on human behaviour; Experiments can give us true knowledge of the human body.

Drawing these at random means students have to be alive to the different parts of whatever topic they have studied. It also creates juxtapositions which might lead students to look at ideas and concepts afresh. For example, if the final statement given above followed the final question, it may cause pupils to discuss the ethics of studying 'medicine in action' and the problems and difficulties which come with such studies.

As an aside, another approach is to give the class the topic which is to be considered and then to distribute a single piece of card to each student. One third of the class could be asked to write a word which links to the topic on their card, one third could be asked to write a question and the final third to write a statement. The teacher could then collect these in, shuffle them and draw them at random for the purposes of the discussion (this method saves the teacher a considerable amount of time).

Extensions and Developments

1. After each mini-discussion (covering whatever is written on the card), the stewards are asked to stand up and find a new partner or group. When they have done this, they draw a new card and begin a new discussion.
2. Challenge students to connect their discussions together, no matter how difficult that may seem to be. Creating continuous connections will cause students to think creatively about the topic and to analyse in depth the various things they talk about.

6. Listening Triad

Explanation

This activity is highly structured. Listening is given great prominence and students get an opportunity to take on a number of roles.

Divide the class into groups of three. Each group must assign the following roles:

- Talker: This person will contribute the most to the discussion. It is their job to talk at length about the topic.
- Questioner: The questioner will make some contributions to the discussion; their main role, however, will be to ask questions of clarification and to prompt the talker.
- Listener: This role requires the student to listen carefully to the discussion and to record the key points. Once the discussion is finished, the listener should feed back to the other group members. They should go over what was talked about in the discussion and provide a peer-assessment of the talker and the questioner.

The teacher will then announce the first discussion topic. Conversations will ensue, with group members taking on their assigned roles. After an appropriate amount of time has passed, the teacher should announce the end of the discussion and ask the listeners to report back to their groups.

Next, group members are asked to rotate roles. A new discussion topic is introduced and conversations recommence. The process continues as above, including a third rotation to ensure each group member gets a turn at each of the roles.

Example

Topic: Human rights

Students get into groups of three and assign roles. The teacher might decide that the following three questions ought to be discussed in turn:

- Should everybody have human rights?
- Do we need a law that protects people's human rights?
- What problems might human rights cause?

Each rotation will see the listener feeding back on the discussion to their colleagues. The advantage of this is twofold. First, by revisiting what was talked about and, hopefully, analysing it, the group will be better placed for the subsequent discussions. This should mean that the quality of the debates increases each time. Second, by providing a peer-assessment of what the talker and the questioner did, the listener is causing the whole group to reflect on what it means to discuss well. Again, this should lead to a progressive improvement in the quality of the discussions.

As can be seen from this example, Listening Triads can be a particularly good way to prefigure a piece of extended writing. The nature of the activity means students will get an opportunity to think, speak, question, listen and reflect on the topic. In addition, a series of notes will be created which can be referred to after the activity has finished.

Extensions and Developments

1. Ask the second and third talkers to make a point of connecting what they say to that which was said previously. Encouraging talkers to contribute in this way will help them to analyse the topic because they will be searching for links between different elements of it. Assign the task of assessing whether connections have been made to the listeners. They should note down each time a connection is made and then relay this to the talkers and questioners at the end of the discussion.

2. The activity bears repetition. Using it time and again across a term, or longer, will help students refine the skills demanded by each role. In so doing they will become ever more adept at the activity and will be increasingly likely to get a lot out of each discussion.

7. Envoys

Explanation

The room is set up so that there are a series of pods, each of which is occupied by a group of three or four students. Pods can simply be two tables pushed together with a collection of chairs around them. Each pod has a task of some sort which the group has to complete. Tasks could include the following:

- A question (or series of questions) which students are to discuss

- An investigation into a collection of resources provided by the teacher
- A selection of resources which students have to read, discuss and summarise
- A discussion centring on the strengths and weaknesses of a specific argument
- A problem which students have to try and solve

Groups are given a set amount of time in which to work together to complete their tasks. All the tasks are linked to the same topic – that which the lesson is about.

When the time is up, one student from each group is nominated as an envoy. They have to leave their pod and join up with another group. On arriving, they must explain what they have been doing and the results of their group's discussion, investigation, problem-solving or whatever. In turn, the group who they have joined must explain to the envoy what they have been doing. After the initial explanation, discussion should ensue. This ought to focus on the similarities and differences between the two groups' experiences as well as the alternative perspectives which can be brought to the different tasks.

The envoys then return to their original groups and discuss what has been found out. The process is repeated as many times as the teacher feels necessary (it is likely that this will be informed by the number of different tasks the teacher has been able to set up).

Example

Topic: How to create effective advertising for food products

The various tasks could be:

- An analysis of the strengths and weaknesses of three examples of food advertising
- A discussion, based around the question: What is the purpose of advertising?
- A rebranding exercise for an existing food item
- An analysis of the strengths and weaknesses of the following argument: 'Different foods require different types of advertising. Therefore, no rules exist which can be applied to all food advertising.'

♦ The creation of a billboard advertisement for a new food product

The tasks themselves will create plenty of discussion, helping students think carefully about the topic and to produce some high-level work. In turn, there will be a lot for the envoys to discuss with other groups and vice versa.

When envoys return to their original groups, both they and their other group members will have been exposed to new ideas. Discussions will thus be twofold. First, they will cover the new ideas. Second, they will deal with the application of these ideas to the particular task which the group was first given.

In the case we have outlined here, an example could be the group who created a billboard advertisement discussing their work in the context of new ideas they have been exposed to regarding the purpose of advertising and the strengths and weaknesses of existing food advertisements.

Extensions and Developments

1. Rotate who is the envoy in each group. This will give different students the opportunity to take their group's ideas out to other members of the class.
2. Challenge students to use what they have come across. This could involve them reworking whatever they produced at the start of the activity (in response to the task) so that it incorporates the new ideas and different perspectives to which they have been exposed by the envoy element of the activity.

8. Jigsawing

Explanation

This task promotes team work and sees students working with a variety of different people. Begin by dividing the class into groups of four. Provide each group with a hand-out. On this there should be a list of four tasks or four questions, all of which will be related to the topic being studied.

Each group should look through the list and discuss the different items on it, though only briefly. They should then decide who in the group is going to be in charge of each item. It will be one task or question per person. Having made the decision, the individual group members should spend around five minutes working independently on their item.

At the end of the allotted time, the teacher announces that the groups are to break up and that new groups should be formed, containing individuals who are all focussing on the same question or task (if this means group sizes which are relatively large, allow two groups per question or task). These new groups then have ten to fifteen minutes to discuss their item in order to reach a conclusion or to successfully complete the task.

Finally, the teacher announces that the original groups are to re-form. These groups will now contain four 'experts' who will be able to explain their findings or results in detail. A discussion can then ensue in which the wider topic is examined through the prisms of the four items or tasks, drawing together all the different ideas which have come up.

Example

Topic: Christian responses to suffering

Each group is provided with a hand-out which contains the following questions:

- What different ways might Christians go about making ethical decisions?
- How might a Christian try to explain the existence of suffering in a world made by God?
- Why might a Christian use the teachings of Jesus to help them work out how they should respond to suffering?
- In what ways might a Christian choose to respond to suffering and why?

The questions have been designed so that they partially overlap but also cover ground of their own. This means there are a range of options which can play to different students' strengths. It also means that in the final discussion (when the original groups re-form) each member of the group will be able to make a unique contribution and that the different contributions will fit together, like a jigsaw, to give an overview of the whole topic.

The teacher might choose to follow up the final discussion with some whole-class feedback, a mini-plenary reflecting on what has been learnt, or a written task in which the different parts of the jigsaw can be brought together and captured in students' books.

Extensions and Developments

1. Increase group sizes to five. This will be challenging for all concerned but will allow each group member to follow a more specialised path. If the logistics can be successfully managed, it is possible that this greater specialisation will lead to each group gaining a more in-depth understanding of the topic as a whole.
2. After the final discussion, ask groups to work together to capture the thinking and discussion which they have done. This could be in the form of a large poster, a report or a presentation.

9. Value Continuum

Explanation

A continuum is a link between two things. It usually spans a large range and often encompasses all possible positions regarding a certain topic. In our case, a value continuum is a link between the two extremes: Strongly Disagree and Strongly Agree. The space in between is the continuous series of points with which an individual could identify, in relation to some statement about values or beliefs.

When used in class, the continuum can be represented by any of the following:

- A double-ended arrow projected or drawn on the board
- A long piece of string or rope either stretched along the floor or suspended at or above head height
- Two pieces of paper stuck to opposing walls, one of which reads, 'Strongly Agree' and the other of which reads, 'Strongly Disagree'

The activity works as follows. Students are presented with the value continuum and the teacher explains what it represents. A statement is then displayed and students are invited to assess where they would place themselves on the continuum, in relation to that statement.

The teacher now has the following options:

- Ask all the students to leave their seats and stand at the point on the continuum which represents their views.
- Ask students to draw the continuum in their books and to mark on it the point which represents their views.
- Give all students a Post-it® note and ask them to write their name on it. Students place the Post-it® note on the continuum at the point which represents their views.

Discussion then ensues. The teacher asks different students to explain the reasons behind their positions, encouraging debate between different members of the class. It may be appropriate to introduce a second and a third statement and to repeat the above process. Doing this will allow the teacher and their students to explore a range of statements concerning a particular topic.

Example

Topic: Shakespeare's *A Midsummer Night's Dream*

The teacher introduces the value continuum and then presents students with the following three statements, each one in turn:

- The play is primarily about the dark side of love.
- The loss of individual identity forms the main theme of the play.
- *A Midsummer Night's Dream* gives us a good insight into Elizabethan norms and values.

For each statement, students are asked to position themselves on the value continuum. The teacher then asks a selection of pupils to explain the reasoning behind their choices. This is used to spark debate, with the teacher encouraging those who occupy different positions on the continuum to defend the reasons behind their choices and to critique the reasons given by other students.

During a debate such as this, it is good to give pupils the opportunity to alter their positions, if they so wish. It may be the case that some of the arguments put forward are sufficiently persuasive to cause a change in a pupil's thinking; they are likely to appreciate the chance to make their position on the continuum reflect such a change.

Extensions and Developments

1. Give students an opportunity to write out a defence of their position prior to them indicating where it lies on the value continuum. This defence could take the form of three separate reasons, each one supported by an example. When it comes to the debate, students will be able to use this written work to support their oral argument (and to raise its quality).

2. Challenge students to occupy a position on the value continuum with which they do not agree and to advocate for that position. While this will be difficult, it will encourage students to think about a viewpoint which is different from their own.

10. Hot-Seating

Explanation

Hot-seating is a dramatic device whereby students are invited to take on the role of a character. This could be a specific person from history, contemporary society or fiction, or it could be a character that is indicative of a group, of a type of person or of a particular job. Examples of the first type would be Napoleon, Barack Obama or Jane Eyre. Examples of the second type would be a member of the working-class in industrial Britain, an extrovert or a town planner.

The purpose of using hot-seating is that the student who takes on the role of a character will be caused to think about the topic from their perspective. In order to do this, they will have to analyse in detail their character's relationship to the topic and then use this to create a convincing portrayal. In essence, they will be interpreting the information about a topic from a point of view which is different to their own.

Two approaches are possible:

1. Choose one student who is to be in the 'hot-seat'. This student comes to the front of the class and is given the details of the character that they are to portray. The rest of the class formulate questions they would like to ask that character. A discussion develops between the student who is in character and the rest of the class.

2. Students are put into groups of four. Each group is given four characters to play. The teacher introduces a statement or question which is to form the basis of discussion. Debate ensues, with students interpreting that which is at issue from the point of view of the character they are playing.

Example

Topic: Renewable energy

The class are looking specifically at wind farms and the impact they can have on the rural environment and the local population. One student is invited to the front of the class and given the character of 'Wind Farm Advocate'. The rest of the class formulate questions based on the various aspects of the issue which have been studied during the lesson (and, perhaps, previous lessons). A debate ensues in which the student who is in the 'hot-seat' has to field the questions which the members of the class ask.

Alternatively, the class could be divided into groups of four and each group given the following roles:

- Wind Farm Advocate
- Government Minister for the Environment
- Leader of the Local Group Against Wind Farms
- Local Farmer

The teacher reveals the statement: 'Wind farms offer considerable benefits to local communities'. Groups discuss this, staying in role as they do. Finally, the teacher may choose to create a whole-class discussion in which the students playing the various roles join up with one another in order to share ideas and arguments.

Extensions and Developments

1. Ask students to identify the characters who they think ought to be role-played in relation to the topic being studied. They should defend their choices with reasons and examples.
2. Develop approach (1) outlined above by having three or four students at the front of the class playing different characters. This will lead to a number of different focus points in the discussion and ensure a wide range of arguments are put forward.

11. Distancing

Explanation

Some topics can be difficult for students to discuss because they themselves are too close to the material or because it evokes feelings and emotions which inhibit free debate. Examples include bullying, bereavement and child poverty. In each of these cases, members of a class may have personal experience of the issue. They may find it difficult to talk about the topic, or to listen to others talk about it, because of the potentially traumatic or distressing experiences they have had.

Situations such as these are a possibility with any group of students. The teacher needs to think in advance about whether any topics which are to be covered are likely to cause difficulties or to have been the subject of negative experiences for their pupils. It will not be possible to predict with total accuracy whether this will have been the case.

Distancing is an approach to discussion which helps make it easier to talk about difficult subjects. It makes it less likely that students will feel upset or that they will feel unable to take part (though it does not wholly remove these possibilities). It involves putting distance between the subject of discussion and the individuals who are discussing it. To do this, the teacher can use methods such as role-play, drama and third-party personal narratives. In each case, the discussion comes to be about the thing which is external (such as the role-play which was performed) rather than that which is internal (personal experience and feelings). This means students are thinking and talking about the issue (including the emotions which go with it) without having to bring in their own ego and experience; their own personality and sense of self is distanced from the issue.

Example

Topic: Bereavement

The teacher makes use of a personal narrative written by a young person but provided through a charity teaching resource (in this case, materials could be taken from the websites of the Child Bereavement Charity or the Red Cross). This is given to students as a hand-out and the class read through it together. Having done so, the teacher asks everyone to think about their own responses before, when they are ready, sharing these with the person sat next to them. The noise level in the room will creep up gradually, with more students feeling comfortable about talking as they hear an increasing number of other voices.

Various questions can be explored from here; the teacher could also introduce a range of activities which supplement the discussion. The key point to remember with this approach is that it involves finding a way to distance the topic from students' personal experience and sense of self. Doing this allows pupils to discuss whatever is at issue and, usually, these topics are the kind of topics which really do need to be discussed.

Extensions and Developments

1. If you decide to capture a distanced discussion in writing, remember that the method is equally appropriate in that medium as well. For example, you could ask students to write about the topic as if they were a particular person other than themselves, or you could ask them to provide general guidelines about the topic for an audience of younger students.
2. You may like to connect together a range of distancing methods in order to help students think about the topic from different perspectives. For example, begin by reading a personal narrative, then conduct some role-play and, finally, ask students to construct their own drama piece. The discussion could stem from the last of these activities, using that which pupils produce as the stimulus for debate.

12. Goldfish Bowl

Explanation

A goldfish swims about in its bowl, all the time visible to anyone who happens to walk past; the glass is no defence against the prying eyes of the world! Goldfish Bowl takes this notion and applies it to discussion. It works as follows:

Students are seated in two concentric circles. We will refer to these as the inner and the outer circles. A topic, question or statement is introduced. This forms the basis of the discussion. The teacher sits in the inner circle and begins the discussion with the students who are also sat in that circle. The students sat in the outer circle listen to the discussion and take notes. These should cover two things: (i) that which is talked about and (ii) the way in which things are discussed.

After sufficient time has elapsed (this will vary depending on the students and what is being debated) the teacher stops the discussion. At this point it is the turn of those students sat in the outer circle. They have been watching and listening to the discussion – looking through the glass of the goldfish bowl, as it were. These pupils should now discuss what has been discussed and how it has been discussed. They should offer contributions which:

+ Demonstrate why comments made by the inner circle were strong or weak.
+ Identify in what direction the discussion is going and suggest whether this is likely to be fruitful or whether a new direction may prove a better option.
+ Highlight areas which have thus far received little coverage.
+ Analyse the general strengths and weaknesses of the discussion up to this point.
+ Suggest ways in which the discussion might be improved.

Following the completion of the outer circle's discussion, the teacher can invite members of the inner and outer circles to swap places. The original discussion then recommences with the roles reversed. Alternatively, the circles may remain as they were, with the inner circle picking up its original discussion and seeking to act on what has been said by the outer circle.

Example

Topic: The ethics of animal research

The class divide into two circles and the teacher introduces the question: 'Is it wrong to experiment on animals?' Students in the inner circle are given a couple of minutes to consider their thoughts on the issue. Meanwhile, the teacher outlines to those pupils sat in the outer circle what it is that they should be looking for in the discussion and the kinds of contributions which will later be expected from them.

The discussion begins with the inner circle, led by the teacher, debating the various arguments which can be made regarding the issue of animal experimentation. Students in the outer circle take notes, based on that which they have been told by the teacher at the start of the discussion. After sufficient time has passed, the first discussion is stopped and the outer circle takes up the baton. The activity then continues as detailed above.

Extensions and Developments

1. Students work in pairs. Each member of the inner circle is paired with the person sat behind them in the outer circle. When the first discussion is stopped, the pairs get together and the member of the outer circle provides feedback to their partner. The discussion starts up again and the member of the inner circle tries to make use of the information which their partner has provided.
2. The inner circle is asked to police its own discussion, or a student-leader is given this task. The teacher then joins the outer circle and shares in their task, listening to and observing the inner circle's discussion and making notes which will be used when it is time for feedback.

13. Freeze-Frame

Explanation

A freeze-frame is a dramatic device. It is a point at which the 'camera' has stopped. The before and after are not seen by the audience, only the moment which has been 'freeze-framed'. It is akin to walking into a room and finding that someone has pressed pause midway through a DVD. You may be able to infer what came before and speculate what will happen next, but your attention is focussed on the moment in time which has been captured.

To use freeze-framing for discussion, begin by arranging the room so that tables are pushed to one side and students, teacher and support staff are sat in a circle of chairs. The teacher should then introduce the topic which is to be discussed. They should talk briefly about this and indicate why it is to be studied and what some of that study might entail. Next, the teacher will present a story or statement which relates to the topic. The whole class will first look at this together. Then, the teacher will divide students into groups of three, four or five.

Groups are given between five and ten minutes to create a freeze-frame which is somehow based on the statement or story which the teacher has presented. While students are working on their drama pieces, the teacher should walk around the room, questioning and giving advice.

Finally, the teacher announces time is up and asks students to sit back down. Either the freeze-frames are showcased in turn, or the teacher chooses a selection for the class to view. After each performance, the group gives an explanation of the thinking which went into their production. Discussion then ensues, with this explanation acting as a starting point. Alternatively, discussion could begin once all the freeze-frames have been shown and explained (with the whole collection acting as stimulus, rather than each one in turn).

Example

Topic: Witchcraft in early modern England

The room is set up as described above and the teacher introduces a narrative of a witch trial at the Old Bailey. This is distributed as a handout and read through by the class as a whole. A few fleeting thoughts are exchanged and the teacher ensures that everyone understands the story and the context from which it comes. Groups are formed and time is given in which to develop and rehearse a freeze-frame.

At the end of this time, students reseat themselves and the teacher asks for a particularly good freeze-frame to be shown to the whole class (they identified this one while walking round during the preparation stages). Let us imagine that the freeze-frame shows a prosecutor pointing at a cowering woman while a hawk-like judge looks on. The thinking behind the performance is then explained by the group.

The combination of the freeze-frame and the explanation provides a wealth of material from which to start a discussion. Students are invited to discuss in their own groups first, before sharing their thoughts with the whole class. The debate continues from there.

Extensions and Developments

1. To ensure that everyone has the opportunity to show their freeze-frame, divide the class in two at the end of the preparation stage. Ask one half to display their freeze-frames

while the other half walk around and observe, then ask students to swap over. A discussion can begin straight after, with students making reference to the performances of their peers.

2. If you have a digital camera and an interactive whiteboard, take photographs of some of the freeze-frames and display these via your computer. This will help students to recall and to talk about different aspects of the performances.

14. Free Discussion

Explanation

Many of the activities outlined here are heavily structured. This is to ensure that students get the most out of discussion and are challenged intellectually in a variety of ways. On occasion, however, it can be stimulating for all involved to have a completely free discussion. This is one in which there is very little structure and the teacher leaves it up to the pupils to determine the course the conversation will take.

A free discussion can begin in one of two ways. It could be that the teacher indicates a topic they think it will be useful for students to talk about, or it could be that the teacher asks their students to propose possible topics for discussion. If the latter option is taken, it may be best to then ask pupils to vote on which option they would like to take up and discuss.

Once the class has settled on a topic, the teacher explains that they will facilitate the discussion, but no more. It will be up to the students themselves to choose how to approach the matter and to decide which areas are most worthy of debate. This may result in a somewhat wayward discussion, perhaps including sections which appear to the teacher to be diversions of a rather tangential nature. Nevertheless, it will be important for them to remain in role as the facilitator and to keep the discussion free from intervention.

Once the debate has been brought to a close, the teacher should lead the class in a self- and peer-assessment exercise. This will cause students to reflect on the discussion and to identify what went well and what could be improved. The results should be noted down and used to inform the next free discussion in which the class engages.

Example

Topic: How do we decide where to site a new nuclear power station?

The activity is self-explanatory. In this case there is a topic suggested by the teacher. Free Discussion is perhaps best used with subject areas which are contentious, open-ended and which incite value judgements. These facets in combination make it more likely that students will be able to talk at length about a topic, without prompting or some sort of structure as an aid.

The self- and peer-assessment should focus on questions such as:

- What did we learn from the discussion?
- What quality of contributions did people make?
- Did we talk about the key issues thrown up by the topic?
- How might we improve the next free discussion we have?
- How has our understanding of the topic altered, as a result of the discussion?

Extensions and Developments

1. Use the self- and peer-assessment to encourage students to think about the purpose of using discussion in the classroom. Ask them to consider how it might be of benefit and what it provides which cannot be accessed through other approaches to learning.
2. Appoint students to certain positions designed to aid the whole class in making the most of their free discussion. These roles could include that of timekeeper, questioner, scribe, leader and summariser.

15. Radio Phone-In

Explanation

This activity uses the set-up of a radio show to create committed, in-depth discussion. Begin by dividing the class into four or five groups and introducing a question which is to be discussed. Give each group a viewpoint regarding the question and explain that they have ten minutes to develop detailed responses from this point of view. Tell the class that at the end of the allotted time, each group will have to send a volunteer up to the front of the class. These volunteers will join the teacher 'on the radio' to discuss the question. Each one will be expected to argue from the viewpoint which their group has been given.

During the preparation period, groups need to do two things. First, they must develop a range of arguments and points which are representative of their viewpoint and which answer the question. They should also identify as much evidence and as many examples as possible which can be used to support their case. Second, they must construct a number of questions which they could 'phone-in' to the radio show, either for their own group member to answer, or for the other volunteers to respond to.

Once the time is up, the volunteers come to the front of the class to join the teacher. It is helpful if a couple of tables are pushed together and then surrounded by chairs (this creates the feel of a radio studio). The teacher sits at the head of the table and takes on the role of radio DJ. They introduce the discussion to the class, explaining what perspectives the various 'guests' are there to represent. A discussion ensues, managed by the host (teacher) and involving the different guests (students). After five minutes or so, the host starts taking questions from the audience (the rest of the class), with these being used to further stimulate and advance the discussion. The activity lasts as long as the teacher chooses; it should become apparent when the debate is beginning to run out of steam. It can be followed up with a written task capturing the various arguments which were put forth (for example, through a compare and contrast table or an essay).

Example

Topic: Is inequality a bad thing?

In this example, the class would be divided into five groups and the following viewpoints would be distributed:

- ◆ Socialism
- ◆ New Labour
- ◆ Traditional conservatism
- ◆ Feminism
- ◆ Anarchism

Groups would spend time preparing points and arguments for their speaker to advance as well as questions to 'phone-in'. Once this time is up, the volunteers would come to the front and the discussion would begin.

In this example, it would be easy for the teacher to facilitate detailed argument between the speakers. It is advisable to choose a range of viewpoints which are likely to be in conflict over what is thought to be the correct answer to the question. This will increase commitment and engagement in the activity.

Questions which might be asked by the audience in this example include:

- (Socialist group to traditional conservatives) How can inequality be a good thing if it results in so many people living their lives in terrible conditions?
- (Feminist group to socialist group) Why do you focus on class inequality and ignore gender inequality?
- (Anarchist group to their own speaker) Can you explain what evidence supports the anarchist position about whether inequality is a bad thing?

Extensions and Developments

1. Ask students to write their questions on pieces of paper and to hand them to the teacher. These can then be drawn out at random and treated as if they were text messages or emails which have been sent in to the radio show.
2. Give members of the audience a peer-assessment pro-forma. Ask them to fill this in as the discussion takes place and to feed back at the end of the activity.

16. Television Chat Show

Explanation

Set the room up as follows: At the front place one chair which is to be the presenter's chair. Next to that, angled-in slightly, place three or four chairs which the 'guests' will come to occupy. Move the tables to one side and arrange the rest of the chairs in two banks, with a space down the middle. The audience will sit in these chairs and the 'guests' will enter by walking between the two banks.

Prior to the lesson, cut up enough pieces of card so that each member of the class will be able to take one piece from you upon entering the room. All but four of these cards should be blank. Two should have 'for' written on them and two should have 'against' written on them. The cards should be handed out face down.

When all the students are seated (in the two banks), ask them to turn their cards over. The four students who have 'for' or 'against' written on their cards will be the 'guests'; the rest will be the audience. Ask the 'guests' to go to the back of the room and then start the show by introducing the proposition which is to be discussed. This should be something which students will already be familiar with and which you are confident they will be able to talk about fairly easily.

Introduce the 'guests' one by one – encourage the audience to clap and cheer as they walk to the front of the room and take up their seats. Once all the 'guests' are sat down, begin asking them about the proposition (the two students who had the 'for' cards will argue in favour of it and the two who had the 'against' cards will argue against it). After a period of discussion between you and the 'guests', start taking questions and points from the audience. Develop the discussion accordingly.

Example

Topic: Analysis of bias in newspaper articles

The teacher sets the room up as detailed above and randomly selects the participants using the card method. Previous lessons have examined how to look for bias in newspaper articles and students are familiar with the topic. With everyone in place, the teacher introduces the show and reveals the statement for debate: 'You can trust most of what you read in newspapers'.

The four students who are playing the role of guests should already be familiar with the arguments around this statement, based on the work the whole class has done in previous lessons. This will ensure the teacher is able to elicit a good discussion from the off. Once this first debate has been conducted, the teacher chooses a range of audience members to either make a contribution to the debate, perhaps developing the arguments which have already been given, or to ask questions of the students who are sat at the front. This format continues until the teacher judges that the discussion is running out of steam.

As is evident, the activity can work especially well towards the end of a unit of work, perhaps prefiguring a written assessment.

Extensions and Developments

1. Print out a picture of a microphone and glue it to a piece of card before cutting it out. Use this to interview audience members. It creates a nice response if the mocked-up microphone is revealed from some sort of hiding place at the point at which the teacher turns their attention from the 'guests' to the audience.

2. If you have sufficient time, collect the cards in at the end of the discussion, shuffle them and redistribute them. Introduce a second proposition which is to be discussed (connected to the same topic as the first one) and instruct the four new 'guests' to come and join you at the front of the room for a new discussion.

17. Post-it® Dialogues

Explanation

This discussion has non-verbal and verbal elements. It requires enough Post-it® notes for everyone in the class (and, ideally, enough so that everyone can have two, three, four or even five).

Begin by explaining to students what the topic for discussion is and why it is an important subject to study. Following this, there are three possible options:

- Project or write one, two or three questions or statements about the topic onto the board.
- Distribute three or four large sheets of paper around the room. Each one should have a question or statement about the topic written on it.
- As above, except instead of distributing the sheets of paper attach them to the classroom walls.

Next, give each student a collection of Post-it® notes. Ask them to consider the various questions or statements. They should then write their responses to these on their notes, before sticking them onto the board or onto the pieces of paper. Once students have done this, ask them to read the various responses which their peers have written. Explain that if they find one of these responses to be particularly interesting they should write their own response to this and stick it underneath the original note.

Ask students to return to their seats. If you have opted for the sheets of paper approach, split the class into three or four groups and hand each one a different sheet of paper. Ask groups to identify the three notes which they feel are of greatest interest. Finally, go round the groups in turn and ask them to share the notes they have identified. Use the comments they read out to stimulate a discussion (depending on how this goes, you may not have time to get round every group).

If you opt for the board approach, you should identify a series of interesting comments yourself and read these out in turn, using each as a starting point for discussion. A good way to begin is by asking the person who wrote the note to explain their thinking and the reasons underpinning the comment they have made.

Example

Topic: The punishment of criminals

The teacher writes the following statements and questions on separate sheets of paper:

- All criminals should be punished for what they have done.
- Punishment is about getting payback.
- Why might punishment lead to more crime?
- Is it a duty to give people a second chance?

These are distributed around the room. Students move about and read the statements and questions. They make their own comments for as many or as few of these as they choose. If they finish this, they go around again and read the comments which other people have left, commenting on these if they so wish.

The teacher then calls time and students return to their seats. The sheets are redistributed and the four groups identify interesting comments. The first group reads out the comment: 'Not all criminals have done bad things – what about people who steal to feed their family?' This point is then elaborated on by the person who wrote it. Other students are invited to make comments and a discussion ensues.

Extensions and Developments

1. If the statements and questions are written on the board and students have stuck the comments up and are seated back at

their desks, you can invite groups of pupils to come up and take away a note which they find interesting (and which is not their own). When everybody has had a chance to do this, the teacher starts the discussion by asking for a volunteer to read out the note they took and to explain why they though it was interesting.

2. Collect the Post-it® notes in, shuffle them, and redistribute them to the class. Pupils then read the note they have been given and discuss it with the person they are sat next to. A whole-class discussion can be developed from this if the teacher so wishes.

18. Rotating Stations

Explanation

Set up six or seven separate stations in your classroom. Each should have something which will stimulate discussion. Examples include:

- A question or statement
- A video or song playing on a laptop
- A collection of sources
- A story or personal narrative
- A series of images
- An object of some kind
- A piece of work produced by a student

In addition to the stimulus material (all of which should link to the main topic), each station should have a large sheet of sugar paper.

When students enter the classroom, divide them into groups of three or four. There should be the same number of groups as there are stations. Give each group a different coloured felt-tip pen. Ask the groups to assign themselves to a station.

When at their station, the groups should investigate the stimulus material and discuss their responses to it. In some cases, it may be necessary to provide a question or a series of instructions to supplement the stimulus material. Once groups have spent time talking they should use their felt-tip pens to write their thoughts on the sugar paper. When the teacher is happy that all groups have done this, they ask pupils to move on to another station and to repeat the process (for ease, ask students to move clockwise around the room).

It is up to the teacher how many rotations they allow (getting groups around every station may be too time-consuming). At the least, you will finish up with sheets of sugar paper with discussion notes written in three or four different colours. These can be used as the basis for a whole-class discussion or for written work which is completed individually or in groups. This activity is particularly good near the start of a topic, as it introduces students to a range of different resources in a short space of time (giving them an introductory overview, as it were).

Example

Topic: The world economy

The teacher has a class of twenty students. They intend to divide the pupils into five groups of four. They might set up stations containing the following material:

- A recent copy of the *Economist* magazine with the question: What can this tell us about the world economy?
- A series of images showing daily life in a developed country and in a developing country.
- The question: Is globalisation a good thing?
- A lump of coal with the question: How might the world economy affect the environment?
- A video charting the recent development of the Chinese economy with the question: How might China's development affect the rest of the world?

Such a set-up will be highly stimulating. There are a range of resources covering many different aspects of the world economy, with these being presented through different mediums. Groups will rotate through the stations, discuss what they encounter and then make notes of their discussions. After the first rotation, groups will also discuss what has already been written at their current station.

On completion of the activity, the teacher will have to decide how to follow it up. They may ask each group to create a report explaining the material and responses at their final station. Alternatively, they may invite students to choose any one of the stations and to write about this at length, with the one proviso being that they must ensure they connect it to the world economy.

Extensions and Developments

1. Create a pro-forma containing the same number of blank boxes as there are stations. Ask students to fill this in as they go around, thus creating their own personal record of the discussions had by their group.

2. Challenge students to rank the stations they visited from most to least relevant. Ask them to explain and defend their choices. This could be extended to a group or whole-class discussion.

19. Think-Pair-Share

Explanation

This activity can stand alone or it can be used within other types of discussion. As a method, its key purpose is to provide a safe, gentle means by which to encourage students to think and talk about a topic. The three processes – think, pair, share – are like three steps, each one leading students a little higher; each one only accessible by climbing the one before.

The teacher asks the class a question or provides a statement to which they are to respond. They then ask students to think silently about the question or statement for between thirty and sixty seconds, making some notes as they do. Next, pupils are asked to team up with the person sat beside them so as to form a pair. These pairs share their thoughts on the question or statement and also share the notes they have made. Working together, they reach a conclusion about what they think the answer is or what they would be happy to share with the rest of the class.

The teacher draws the whole class back together and asks a number of different pairs to share their thoughts. These are used to stimulate a discussion about the original question or statement. Everyone is able to take part because of the prior work they have done thinking, talking and writing about that which is at issue.

Example

Topic: Impressionism in art

The teacher presents students with the question: If an artist is painting in an impressionist style, what might they be trying to achieve? This is thought and written about individually, then discussed in pairs before being debated as a whole class.

Extensions and Developments

1. Extend the amount of time given for the thinking section of the activity; ask students to write at length about the question or statement. This will provide them with a greater amount of material to discuss with a partner. It will also be possible for partners to swap their work, read through what the other person has written and then discuss their thoughts on this.

2. Insert a task between the 'pair' and 'share' processes. Using our example from above, this might entail asking pairs to come up with a short guide to the purposes behind the use of impressionism. Such a development takes advantage of the rapport built up between partners. It also ensures pairs have a product informing the contributions they make in the 'share' process.

20. Three-Step Interview

Explanation

The teacher introduces a question, statement or some stimulus material. Students are divided into groups of four. In each group, pupils are labelled A, B, C and D. The discussion works as follows:

Step One: Student A interviews Student B. Student C interviews Student D. The interviews aim to elicit what the students think about the question, statement or stimulus material. Student A and Student C take notes while they conduct their interviews.

Step Two: Student B interviews Student A. Student D interviews Student C. The interviews aim to elicit what the students think about the question, statement or stimulus material. Student B and Student D take notes while they conduct their interviews.

Step Three: The group re-forms as a four. Each student takes it in turn to relay to the group the thoughts and ideas of the person they interviewed, using their notes to help them. Interviewees are allowed to add anything which they think has been missed (or misrepresented) by their interviewer. Once each student has had the opportunity to give feedback, the group discuss the question, statement or stimulus material as a whole.

Ideally, this will involve students picking up on things which have been said by their colleagues and further debating these.

Example

Topic: Product design

The teacher asks students the following question: Is it better to use sustainable materials or the materials which create the best product? A short period of thinking time is given and then the class is divided into groups of four. The students in each group assign the labels A, B, C and D to themselves. The interview process takes place as outlined above.

It may be that, during their interview, Student B indicates that they think the best product will be the one which is sustainable. Upon hearing this during step three, Students C and D may disagree, taking issue with the way in which Student B has understood the term 'best'. After all the interviewers have relayed what was said by their interviewees, Students C and D could follow this up, asking Student B to explain how exactly they have interpreted the word 'best'. The discussion would carry on from here, sparked off by a specific comment made during the interview process.

Extensions and Developments

1. Ask students to come up with a list of questions they will use in their interviews. These could be based around some stimulus material provided by the teacher, or simply a general topic or concept.
2. Try the activity with groups of six (although be aware that it might be difficult to manage). Label students A, B, C, D, E and F. Take them through the same three-step process; the main difference will be that three pairs of interviews take place instead of two. This can create more possibilities for group discussion during the final part of step three.

CHAPTER FOUR

Twenty More Activities

In this chapter we look at a further twenty activities, all of which can be used to structure discussion. Each one is explained, exemplified and supplemented by extensions and developments.

Every activity is practical, effective and ready to use. Each one can be tailored to work with nearly all areas of the curriculum and most age groups.

1. Silent Debate

Explanation

This is a non-verbal, whole-class discussion. An oral element can be added to the end of the activity if the teacher so wishes. It works as follows:

The teacher must prepare in advance four or five large sheets of paper. The number will be determined by how many students there are in the class. Each sheet of paper should have a statement or question written in the middle of it. This should connect to the current area of study.

During the lesson, or at the beginning, the teacher explains to the class that they will be taking part in a silent debate. The rules are as follows:

- No talking
- Contributions must be written

Anyone who is caught talking is sent to the 'naughty corner' for thirty seconds before being allowed to re-join the debate.

The sheets of paper are distributed around the room. The teacher should make sure that they are reasonably far away from one another. Students are instructed to equip themselves with a pen or a pencil and to stand up and walk around the room. It is explained that they should visit each of the sheets of paper and read the questions or statements which are written on them. Having done so, they should write a response on a blank section of the paper, explaining what they think about the point at issue.

Once students have commented on all the sheets of paper they are to walk around the room a second time. On this journey they will be reading the comments which other pupils have written. They should comment on these comments by first circling them, then drawing a line, then writing their own thoughts at the end of this line before circling what they have written. The end effect will be a clear, visual representation of an exchange of views.

The teacher keeps the activity going for as long as they feel is appropriate. Students are allowed to keep writing comments until the teacher says otherwise.

If the teacher chooses, they can add an oral element at the end of the activity. This involves handing the written-on sheets to various sections of the class and asking them to identify two or three particularly interesting comments. These are read out and a discussion ensues, with this being started by the person who originally wrote the comment.

Example

Topic: Identity

The teacher might choose the following questions and statements for their sheets of paper:

- How important is identity?
- What exactly is an identity?
- A person's identity is decided by what other people think about them.
- People's identities stay the same over time.
- Do we only have one identity?

These have been designed with discussion in mind. All of them invite a number of different responses and all of them are fairly open. They will provoke a range of comments from members of the class. This will result in sheets which are covered in writing, demonstrating sustained and engaged thinking about the topic.

Extensions and Developments

1. Use the activity at the start of a unit of work. When the task has been completed, take the sheets of paper and stick them up on the wall. These can then be referred to and reviewed during future lessons.

2. Use the activity at the start of a topic. Keep the sheets which are produced. At the end of the unit, repeat the activity using exactly the same questions and statements. Compare and contrast the two sets of responses and ask students to analyse how studying the topic has affected their thinking.

2. Café Culture

Explanation

This activity takes its inspiration from continental café-style culture. The room is set up in a series of pods. These are made up of one or two tables with four or five chairs around them. Each pod is equipped with a sheet of A3 paper and a pen. The number of pods you have will be determined by the number of students in your class. Ideally, you will want no more than four students at each pod at any one time.

Pupils distribute themselves around the room, sitting at the pods. The teacher explains what topic the class is studying and why it is to be studied. In advance of this, they will need to have prepared the same number of slips of paper as there are pods. Each of these slips should have written on it a question or statement that relates to the topic of study.

The teacher hands out the slips of paper, one to each pod. The student who is chosen to receive the paper is in charge of that pod. They write the question or statement at the top of their piece of paper. Students are then invited to discuss the point at issue in their pods, with the person who is in charge making notes on the sheet of paper. After four or five minutes, the teacher announces that all students except those who have been placed in charge should stand up and move to another pod.

Once students are in their new groupings, the person in charge explains what the question or statement is and what has previously been discussed. They use the notes made on the sheet of paper as an aid to their explanation. The groups then pick up the discussion from where it was left off and take it in whatever direction they wish.

The whole process is repeated as many times as the teacher feels is appropriate. It may be helpful to swap over the people in charge of the pods so as to avoid boredom or frustration setting in.

Example

Topic: World War II

The class have already studied the build-up to World War II. The teacher explains that they are to continue studying this but that the lesson will focus on the application of existing knowledge along with analysis and assessment of different interpretations. There are twenty-four students and so the teacher arranges the room into six pods. They give out six slips of paper containing the following statements and questions:

- The Treaty of Versailles was the direct cause of World War II.
- How important was Hitler's personality in causing the war?
- There was no way that war could have been averted.
- If there had not been a Great Depression in the 1930s, World War II would not have happened.
- Why did the war not start sooner?
- How might nationalist ideology be said to have caused the war?

Students move between various pods, discussing a number of the statements and questions. In so doing they are thinking carefully about their existing knowledge of the topic as well as refining their understanding. In addition, the thinking they are being asked to do is at a high level; it involves evaluation, analysis, assessment and synthesis.

In this particular example, the activity would serve as an excellent partner to an essay-writing task. If this was to be the case, the sheets of paper could be stuck up at the front of the room for students to refer to as they go about writing their essays.

Extensions and Developments

1. At the end of the activity ask the students who are in charge of each pod to share their final thoughts regarding their question or statement with the whole class.

2. If you have a computer and an interactive whiteboard, project an image of a street café and play some incidental music. This will help create the atmosphere of a continental café in which people are meeting to discuss the big issues of the day.

3. Analyst's Couch

Explanation

This activity mimics the set-up of a consulting room without making direct use of the methods of psychoanalysis; students are invited to analyse their opinions, arguments and interpretations rather than their unconscious mind!

The teacher begins by introducing a statement related to the topic of study. They then ask students whether they agree or disagree with this. Some time is given for pupils to think about their responses and to write down an argument, or a series of points, which they would put forward in relation to the statement.

Having done this, pupils are asked to pair up with the person sat next to them and to arrange their chairs such that one of the two is sat slightly behind and to the side of the other (akin to how an analyst might sit with their patient). The student who is sat in the chair which is further back is to take on the role of analyser.

The activity begins with the pupil who is sat further forward outlining to their partner their argument regarding the statement. While they are doing this, the 'analyser' should listen carefully, making notes if necessary. At the end of the explanation, the 'analyser' should start asking their partner questions about the argument they have put forward. These questions should be designed to make them think carefully about what they have said and to examine the premises, implications and logical extents of that which they have proposed.

Once this exchange has been exhausted, students swap positions and repeat the activity with the roles reversed. The result should be that both students are caused to think in detail about the nature of the arguments they have outlined. It is expected that thinking about them in this way will also cause them to refine them. If the teacher wishes, a whole-class discussion could follow (or the activity could be combined with Value Continuum).

Example

Topic: Interpreting poetry

The teacher puts the following statement on the board: 'The poetry of Wordsworth is best explored through the emotions it evokes.' Students are invited to think about this statement and to note down their own responses, forming these into an argument or a series of points. Either way, pupils should explain why they agree or disagree with the statement.

Students then get into pairs, arrange their chairs as indicated above and the one who is sat further forward outlines their thoughts. The 'analyser' then asks questions along the following lines:

- What other arguments could one put forward and why have you chosen not to advocate these?
- On what premises does your argument rest?
- What are the implications of your argument for (i) reading Wordsworth; (ii) writing about the poetry of Wordsworth; and (iii) analysing poetry in general?
- What are the weak points in your argument? Why do they exist? Can you do anything about them?
- What evidence might someone use to challenge your argument? How would you meet that challenge?

It may be that, at first, the teacher will need to model the kind of questions the 'analyser' is expected to ask. Another option is to provide generic questions (like those detailed above) which can be adapted to the specific statement under consideration.

Extensions and Developments

1. Once students have been through the analysis process, ask them to rewrite their arguments and to then repeat the activity. In the second running they should be able to put into practice

the improvements they have made as a result of the first run through.

2. As students get comfortable with the activity, encourage more of a dialogue between the 'analyser' and their partner. This could involve the 'analyser' not just asking questions but also putting forward their own views about their partner's argument, with a dialogue developing as a result of this.

4. Select Committee

Explanation

Select Committees are made up of groups of MPs or members of the House of Lords. The House of Commons has Select Committees for each department of government as well as some cross-departmental committees. The House of Lords has fewer committees which focus on specialist areas, taking advantage of the specific expertise of members of that House and the greater amount of time available to them for examining issues.

The committees review information and interview individuals who are called or required to attend. They produce reports for public consumption based on specific remits. Here is how to use Select Committees as a medium for discussion:

Set up the classroom as follows: arrange a number of tables in a horseshoe and place eleven chairs around them. At the open end of the horseshoe place two tables and four chairs. Place the remaining chairs behind these in rows of five.

Explain to students what topic, question or statement will form the focus of the debate. Choose eleven pupils to be on the Select Committee. They will go off and research the topic, question or statement, finding out as much as they can before the time is up. The remaining students will all be playing the role of individuals or groups who have been called to give evidence before the Select Committee. The teacher will need to plan in advance who these are to be. They will also need to provide resources which the students can use to inform themselves about the views and opinions of these people. With roles assigned, the resources are handed out. Pupils familiarise themselves with these before the teacher calls time.

Select Committee members take their seats at the horseshoe. The rest of the students sit on the chairs assembled in rows. The teacher hands the head of the Select Committee (sat at the top of the horseshoe) a list of the individuals and groups who are to be called to give evidence. They are called in whatever order is desired and sit at the two tables and four chairs at the open end of the horseshoe. Evidence is a combination of speeches and the answering of questions posed by the Select Committee members. Those giving evidence can discuss and debate with the Select Committee members if the opportunity presents itself.

Once everyone has been called to give evidence, students rearrange the room and write their own report on the topic, taking into account the proceedings of the Select Committee.

Example

Topic: Cloning

The teacher explains that the Select Committee will be examining whether human cloning should be made legal in the United Kingdom. The students who will form the Select Committee are sent off to research the topic (it is presumed that some preparatory work has already been done in a previous lesson). The remainder of the students are given various roles to play. Let us imagine that in this case there are fifteen other students who are given the following roles:

- Three are asked to play representatives of the Catholic Church.
- Three are asked to play representatives of a pro-cloning private scientific research company.
- Three are asked to play representatives of a university research department which specialises in human illness and disease.
- Three are asked to play representatives of the Church of England.
- Three are asked to play representatives of the British Medical Association.

Each group is given resources with which they are to familiarise themselves. They can also take these with them to the Select Committee if they so wish.

While the students investigate the roles they will be playing, the teacher gives the head of the Select Committee a list of who will be called to give evidence. This gives that group of students the opportunity to frame some questions in advance.

With preparation time at an end, the discussion takes place as outlined above, each group being called in turn to give evidence.

Extensions and Developments

1. Give members of the Select Committee slips of paper on which is written a position regarding that which is being investigated. Members keep this secret but use it to inform their questioning and discussion contributions. This will help ensure a range of views are heard during the main part of the activity.

2. Allow members of the Select Committee to recall individuals and groups if they have further questions for them. This gives members the opportunity to think about what is discussed during the activity and to consider whether it throws up new issues or perspectives which were not previously covered.

5. Question Time

Explanation

This activity is based on the long-running BBC television programme of the same name. It is best used when the topic under consideration can be interpreted from a series of distinct perspectives.

The teacher introduces the topic which is to form the basis of the activity. Ideally, students should have had a few previous lessons on this and, therefore, should be familiar with the ins and outs of the subject. Five students are chosen (or volunteer) to be the guests on the Question Time panel. The teacher gives each of these students a perspective from which they must argue. The pupils are sent to the far side of the room to make notes on how their perspectives interpret the topic.

The remainder of the class are put into groups of three or four and invited to identify different areas of the topic which could be discussed. Once they have done this, they are asked to formulate questions based on these areas and to write the questions on slips of paper distributed by the teacher. Finally, the slips of paper are collected in and the class rearranges the room as follows:

Three tables are placed at the front of the room with six chairs. The rest of the chairs are set out in rows, facing the three tables and six chairs. The teacher sits in the middle of the three tables, with the five student guests sat either side. The rest of the class sit on the remaining chairs; they are the audience.

The teacher introduces the guests, explaining what perspective each one is representing, and then pulls out a question at random from the collected slips of papers. Members of the panel are invited to discuss the question, taking it in turns to share their views. The person whose turn it is to speak is indicated by the teacher (who is the host). Once a little time has elapsed, contributions are invited from the audience. The discussion continues in this manner, with the teacher picking out more questions at random and these being discussed by the panel and the audience.

Example

Topic: The sociology of crime

Five students volunteer to be guests on the Question Time panel. They are given the following theoretical perspectives:

- Marxism
- Feminism
- Functionalism
- Postmodernism
- Interactionism

They all go to the far side of the room (so they do not hear the questions students come up with) and analyse how their perspectives interpret crime in society. The remainder of the class identify areas of the sociology of crime which could be discussed and formulate questions based on these areas.

The teacher collects the questions in, the room is rearranged and the discussion begins. Let us imagine that the first question drawn out by the teacher is: 'What explains why crime happens in society?' This will provide plenty of scope for each of the guests to talk from their own perspective. It will also generate disagreement because of the various positions the guests have been asked to uphold. Audience members will then be able to bring in their own perspectives, which will not be beholden in the same way that those of the guests are. A high-quality, analytical discussion should ensue. The teacher moves the class on to the next question when they feel the time is right.

Extensions and Developments

1. When playing the role of the host, the teacher can take on various dispositions. For example: amiable, inquisitorial, combative, contrary and conciliatory. These could all be called on at different times, depending on the present state of the discussion.
2. Invite members of the audience to respond directly to comments made by members of the panel. This will help generate debate about the perspectives or interpretations which are informing the comments put forward by the guests.

6. What If...?

Explanation

This activity is all about speculation. It encourages students to discuss possibilities and to imagine what might be the case. In so doing, it challenges them to reason from existing premises and evidence and to think creatively. There can sometimes be tension between these two aims; 'What If...?' offers an opportunity to weave them together.

The activity can be conducted with a whole class, in pairs or in groups. A general outline follows, succeeded by suggestions of how it might be tailored to each one of these set-ups.

The teacher identifies a concept or an aspect of the topic which students would benefit from exploring in some detail. They craft a number of 'What if...?' scenarios from this. These are hypothetical situations which cause students to think carefully about their existing knowledge of the concept or aspect of the topic. This is so that they can imagine what the consequences of the stated hypothesis might be; the suggestions which are put forward are debated, tested and examined through discussion.

Whole-class set-up: The teacher projects or writes a 'What if...?' hypothesis onto the board. Students are given thinking time before being asked to share their thoughts with the person next to them. The teacher then asks individual students to share their ideas with the whole class. A discussion ensues in which various suggestions are heard. The arguments underpinning these are examined, debated and tested.

Paired set-up: The teacher projects or writes three 'What if…?' hypotheses onto the board. Students work in pairs to come up with a range of suggestions for each one. They identify what they believe to be their most likely, well-reasoned or creative suggestions for each and join up with another pair to discuss these.

Group set-up: Students get into groups of three or four. Each group is given a hand-out containing a 'What-if…?' scenario. Ideally, each group's scenario should be different. Students discuss the 'What if…?' they have been given; different suggestions are put forward and debated by the group. Eventually, a decision is made as to which suggestion is deemed the best. An extended argument is developed, explaining why the group thinks it likely that this suggestion would come to be the case. The teacher brings the class back together and each group in turn shares what they have produced. The whole class discusses each of these answers, debating, testing and challenging the arguments different groups put forward.

Example

Topic: The legal system

The most important part of this activity is developing good questions; fitting them into the whole-class, paired or group set-ups outlined above is fairly straightforward.

Here is a selection of 'What if…?' questions which could be used in conjunction with the topic of the legal system:

- What if there were no laws?
- What if trials took place behind closed doors?
- What if politicians were allowed to appoint judges?
- What if the police announced that they were going to stop dealing with minor crimes and only concentrate on major ones?
- What if the government redefined theft so that it only counted if goods of fifty pounds or more were stolen?
- What if it was made illegal to send people to prison?
- What if company owners were made legally responsible for helping people they sacked get a new job?

As you will note, such questions can be specific or general, likely or unlikely. The key point is to identify scenarios which will cause students to discuss the concept or aspect of the topic critically and creatively. For example, the sixth question, about prison, is unlikely to ever be the case. What it does, though, is to cause students to think about the concepts of justice and punishment, as well as the punitive functions of the criminal justice system.

Extensions and Developments

1. Invite students to come up with their own 'What if…?' questions. The teacher may need to set some boundaries or success criteria through which to direct students' thoughts. This can work particularly well if set as a homework task. The next lesson can then begin with pupils posing their questions to each other or to the whole class.

2. In the group set-up outlined above, the teacher might choose to add a drama element. This would see each group dramatizing the suggestion they have agreed on. Performances could then be shown to the rest of the class and paired up with the detailed arguments each group will have developed.

7. Socratic Dialogue

Explanation

Socrates was an ancient Greek philosopher. No writings of his survive; he is known to us through the writings of his pupil, Plato. In Plato's books, the character of Socrates engages in discussion with many other individuals. His general method is to question the assumptions, concepts and categories upon which the opinions and beliefs of these other people rest. Socrates' purpose is not to patronise others or to make himself look better than them, rather, he is in search of truth, understanding, consistency and clear thinking. He wants to encourage these traits in others and to demonstrate the extent to which we assume certainty or correctness where, in fact, we do not have good cause to. In essence, Socrates is a philosopher.

We will outline here how Socratic dialogue can be put into practice in the classroom. The best advice, however, is to read some of Plato's work in order to see the method in its original form. *Crito* and *Euthyphro* are good places to start.

A question is posed. This can be to do with anything, although questions of a philosophical nature work particularly well. Examples of such questions include:

- Questions concerning morality
- Questions concerning concepts and categories
- Questions concerning the status of knowledge
- Questions concerning the nature of reality
- Questions concerning aesthetics

Students are given time to reflect on the question and to gather their thoughts. If it is warranted, the teacher may opt to give students an extended period of time in which to work on the question.

The dialogue itself can either be teacher-led or student-led.

Teacher-led: The teacher chooses a student to begin the discussion. They share their response to the question. The teacher uses the four Socratic techniques outlined earlier in this book (ignoramus, midwife, gadfly and stingray) to question and probe the student's answer. A dialogue takes place between teacher and student with the rest of the class listening. The teacher's aim is, through questioning, to encourage the pupil to analyse in detail the propositions, concepts, categories, premises and assumptions which their belief, opinion or argument rests on. The teacher may choose to stay in dialogue with that one student, or to open dialogues with a number of other students. The opportunity may also arise to bring in other pupils to further question the original student, or to offer support for what it is they are arguing.

Student-led: As above, except students work in groups and one person takes on the role of the questioner. This will require greater preparation as pupils will need to familiarise themselves with how to question and probe appropriately. In this form the activity is best used repeatedly; students will quickly improve their performances as a result.

Example

Topic: How to write up an experiment

The teacher might pose the question: What is the best way to write up an experiment? Students are given time to think about this and to formulate an answer. The teacher chooses someone to begin the discussion. They comment: 'The best way to write up an experiment is to follow a structure and to make sure you include everything which happened.'

Such a comment invites many questions. Concentrating only on the concept of structure, we could ask the following:

- What do you mean by a 'structure'?
- What is the benefit of using a structure? What is it exactly that a structure does?
- In this case, what specific structure do you have in mind? Why that structure? Could an alternative structure be used?
- What limitations might one encounter when using a structure?
- If someone was to write up their experiment without using a structure, why would that be a bad thing? Could it not be the case that by avoiding using a structure one might throw up alternative readings of the data or different ways of thinking about the experiment?

As can be seen from these examples, the purpose is to get beneath the surface of language and thought, to interrogate the foundations upon which our statements, propositions and arguments rest. This leads us to the two greatest benefits of Socratic discussion: (i) it encourages students to think critically and (ii) it causes students to look more deeply at what they think and to question the legitimacy of those thoughts. They are thus led toward better understanding and improved reasoning.

Extensions and Developments

1. If the student-led method is used, the teacher can walk around the room and look for particularly good examples of Socratic dialogue. The students involved in one of these could then give a performance for the whole class at the end of the activity. This will provide a good model for other pupils to follow.

2. Create exemplar sheets for students which explain the roles of ignoramus, midwife, gadfly and stingray. Each could be supplemented by a picture (to aid memory) and a set of generic

questions. Students can then have these to hand when doing their own Socratic dialogues.

8. Job Interview

Explanation

This activity is best used towards the end of a unit of work. Students work in groups of four. Each group needs a table and four chairs. Three of the chairs are placed on one side of the table, opposite the remaining chair. Students sit down. Those sat in the group of three chairs are the interview panel. The pupil who is left is the job applicant.

Prior to the 'interview rooms' being set up, the teacher explains to the class that a number of students will be applying for jobs as experts in whatever the topic is that has been studied over the past few weeks. The class is then divided into groups of four. Each group must nominate a job applicant. These pupils all leave their groups and sit together. They are given ten minutes or so to go over what they have been learning in recent weeks.

The rest of the class are tasked with coming up with interview questions. The teacher explains that the purpose of the interview will be to generate a discussion through which the panel can assess whether their applicant really is an expert in the field. Questions should thus be open and will be followed up with contributions, comments and further questions by the panel.

When the time is up, groups re-form, arranging the interview set-up as outlined above. Interviews commence, with the panel members taking it in turns to ask questions and to discuss answers with the job applicant.

Example

Topic: Shakespeare's *Macbeth*

In this example, let us imagine that students have been studying *Macbeth* for a number of weeks. As a result, they will all be familiar with the play and should have spent plenty of time analysing, interpreting and evaluating it.

The class is put into groups and job applicants are identified. They go off to one side of the room in order to prepare. The remainder of the class come up with questions, based on the premise of generating discussion and eliciting knowledge and understanding.

With this in mind, good questions would include ones such as:

- What do you feel are the most important themes in the play?
- In your opinion, what characterises the relationship between Macbeth and Lady Macbeth?
- What does the play suggest about the nature of ambition?

Bad questions would be ones such as:

- Who killed Duncan?
- How many witches are in the play?
- What is the name of Banquo's son?

The risk with this activity is that students will ask factual, knowledge-based questions such as these. Such questions will stimulate little discussion. It is therefore important to stress that the questions ought to elicit discussion and should be a point from which the job applicant and the interview panel can start to talk to one another. In some cases, it may be necessary to model such questions.

Extensions and Developments

1. After the interviews are completed, ask the job applicants to stand up and join another interview panel. A second interview commences; the level of discussion should be better as students will already have had a first attempt.
2. Swap the roles of job applicant and interviewer. This will allow some students to experience both sides of the activity.

9. Examination Committee

Explanation

For this activity, the teacher needs to have available a number of pieces of work which were produced by students and which are based on the topic currently being studied. This might take the form, for example, of work created by the previous cohort of students when they were studying the topic. The selection chosen should encompass a variety of grade levels and, if possible, a series of different approaches to whatever task or question was set. It should be photocopied so that there are enough copies for each group.

The purpose of the activity is for students to discuss the work and to use a mark-scheme in order to assess its standard. The benefits are threefold. First, students will be talking at length about the topic, making use of what they have learnt so as to make judgements about the work in front of them. Second, students will get to see a variety of different responses to a question or task. This will provide them with some reference points regarding how they themselves might seek to engage with the topic. Third, they will spend time discussing and using an appropriate mark scheme. This will help them to become familiar with how their own work will be marked and to identify what is required to achieve highly.

The class is divided into groups of three or four. The teacher explains the task (to read through the work and discuss it, then to read through the mark-scheme and to apply this through discussion to the work). Copies of the work and the mark-scheme are handed out. Students are given between fifteen and twenty-five minutes to complete the task (the time it takes can vary considerably). The teacher may wish to create a whole-class discussion at the end. This would involve a few of the pieces of work being talked through in turn, with groups sharing their thoughts and what marks they awarded and why.

Example

Topic: The repeal of the Corn Laws

Let us imagine that, the year previous, students in Year 11 wrote an essay entitled 'What factors led to the repeal of the Corn Laws?' Five copies of this are photocopied by the teacher. They include two essays which scored highly, two which scored in the middle of the scale and one which scored lowly. The names of the students who wrote these essays are obscured (if they have been written on the originals) to ensure anonymity.

Each group receives a copy of these five essays along with two copies of the GCSE History mark-scheme for extended written answers. Students begin by reading through the essays and then discussing them as a group. They then read through the mark-scheme and use it to formally assess the essays. Next, the group discusses the application of the mark-scheme to the essays; the teacher makes it a precondition that agreement must be reached for all essays before a group can claim that they have finished the task.

When the teacher decides time is up, they can lead a whole-class discussion, looking at each one (or a selection) of the essays in turn. Another alternative is to combine the activity with Envoys. In this case, one student would leave each group, join up with another group and compare the marks which each decided to award.

Extensions and Developments

1. At the end of the activity, ask students to reflect in their groups on the difficulties of using mark-schemes as well as the benefits they can provide.
2. Challenge students to highlight examples of good practice in each essay, to connect these to specific parts of the mark-scheme and to offer a reasoned defence of why these are particularly strong elements of the work in question.

10. Viva

Explanation

A viva, or viva voce, is an oral examination, usually undertaken by PhD students and also used in some other educational settings. It involves one or more examiners asking a candidate questions so as to assess their knowledge and understanding of a subject. It is sometimes taken as a standalone examination, sometimes in addition to a written paper or submission. For our purposes, that is, applying its premises to the classroom, it is not dissimilar to Job Interview. There are sufficient variations, however, for it to warrant its own entry.

The activity is best used towards the end of a topic. It could form the basis of an oral peer-assessment, the results of which would contribute to the teacher's holistic assessment of pupil progress. The task requires students to be fairly knowledgeable about the topic in question. After all, they are going to be setting and answering questions concerning that particular subject.

The teacher explains to the class that they will be working in pairs. Six aspects of the topic are projected or written onto the board. These will form the basis of the examination questions. In each pair, Student A is given the first three aspects and Student B the second three.

Pupils then have between five and ten minutes to develop a range of questions for each of their aspects. The emphasis should be on open questions which will allow the person answering to talk at length and for discussion to develop between them and the 'examiner'.

Finally, each pair is invited to find a space in the room where they can sit facing one another. The teacher indicates that Student A will begin as the 'examiner' and that Student B will need to answer their questions for a set length of time (this will depend on the particular class and is for the individual teacher to decide). When this time is up, the roles are reversed. Stress the importance of discussion and make it clear that the examiner should follow up on the answers they receive so as to generate critical and engaged talk.

Example

Topic: Ethical decision-making

Students are presented with the following six aspects of the topic (it is a Religious Studies unit of work):

- Rules and rule-following
- Christianity
- Values
- Consequences
- Islam
- Utilitarianism

Student A is given the first three and Student B is given the second three. If the teacher thought it appropriate, they could provide a sample question for each aspect. This would act as a model for students and help them to get started in writing their own questions. In our example we might use the following:

- Is following rules a good way to make ethical decisions, no matter the circumstances?
- What are the strengths and weaknesses of the different methods of ethical decision-making available to Christians?

◆ Is any single value more important than all others? Is this true universally, or just for yourself?

◆ If we cannot predict the future, is there any point thinking about the consequences of our actions?

◆ Why might Muslims encounter difficulties when interpreting the guidance offered by the Qur'an?

◆ What is happiness and is there such a thing as overall happiness?

Each student would be able to take their three questions as a starting point, supplementing these with another couple of their own. They would then use these in the activity when it is their turn to play the role of the examiner.

Extensions and Developments

1. At the end of the activity, ask all the Student Bs to remain seated. All Student As swap places. The activity is repeated with the new pairings. It is likely that the timings for this second activity will be reduced; pupils will be more familiar with the material and will not need as long to think.

2. Give students a peer-assessment pro-forma. Ask them to fill this out while they are playing the role of the examiner. At the end of the activity students exchange their completed pro-forma and discuss the results.

11. Round-Table

Explanation

Round Table is a fairly unstructured discussion activity in which students take the lead. In terms of numbers, the following is suggested:

Under 10 students = 1 group

10 to 20 students = 2 or 3 groups

20 to 30 students = 3 or 4 groups

The deciding factor will be the extent to which the teacher can rely on their students to self-regulate. The bigger the group size, the more important self-regulation will be. It is a balancing act; small group sizes (which are easier for the teacher to monitor closely) may not provide sufficient input to ensure good discussion.

The activity works as follows:

Book a computer room or a set of laptops in advance. Introduce students to the topic which is to be studied. Divide the class into groups in line with the numbers suggested above. Split each group into pairs. Provide a range of areas which form part of the lesson topic. Ask each pair to select an area. No group should have two pairs selecting the same area.

Pairs are then asked to research their area using the internet. Specifically, they are to identify one article, story or report which connects to their area. They should print this off and prepare the following:

+ A summary of the article, story or report
+ A brief explanation of why they thought it was interesting
+ A question to pose to their peers, inspired by the item

Pairs return to their original groups. They push three tables together and sit around these. They take it in turns to summarise their item and to explain its relevance. They then pose their question and the group has a round-table discussion about this. The activity continues until each pair's question has been discussed.

As can be inferred, this activity works particularly well at the beginning of a topic; it gets students actively engaged with various aspects of a new area of study.

Example

Topic: Climate change

The teacher may present the following areas and ask students to select an option:

+ Causes
+ Consequences
+ Impact on humans
+ Impact on animals and wildlife
+ Solutions
+ Politics
+ Data
+ Charities and NGOs

It is as well to provide more options than there are pairs in each group. This will help to avoid clashes over who gets to choose which area.

In our example here, students would get into groups, then into pairs and then choose an option which they would use the internet to research. Let us imagine that Pair A selects 'Solutions' and finds a newspaper article about wind energy. They would print this off, summarise it, and discuss why they believe it to be interesting.

When the groups re-form, Pair A present their article before asking their question. This could be something such as: 'How might we encourage the government to invest in wind energy?' The group then discuss this question. Each pupil would be able to bring in ideas and information they have come across in their own researches. Once the discussion has been exhausted, Pair B takes over from Pair A and so on until everyone has had their turn.

Extensions and Developments

1. Challenge students to choose an aspect of the topic about which they have little or no prior knowledge. This will make researching more difficult but also more rewarding.
2. Ask students to write a summary of their discussion. They should use this to identify any areas they feel are worthy of further study. Any choices should be justified.

12. Speed Debating

Explanation

Present students with a proposition related to the topic of study. Divide the class in two. Explain that one half of the class will be arguing in favour of the proposition and the other half will be arguing against it. Give students fifteen minutes in which to develop a series of arguments they can use to defend their position and to critique the position of their opponents. This is best done with the two sets of students sat on opposite sides of the room. It is important, however, to avoid having two very large groups working together (as many students will struggle to participate). Instead, split each half of the class into smaller groups, but allow ideas to be shared. Here is an illustration:

There are twenty-four students in a class.

Twelve are to argue 'for' and twelve are to argue 'against'.

Each set of twelve is split into three groups of four.

The groups of four work together and develop their arguments.

Groups are allowed to exchange ideas with one another if they wish.

While pupils are developing their arguments, the teacher rearranges the room. It should be set up so that there is a line of tables with an equal number of chairs either side. Continuing our example, we would have six tables with twelve chairs either side. The chairs are turned so that they face one another across the tables.

When the time is up, the teacher asks the group of students who are in favour of the proposition to sit on the chairs lined up on one side of the tables. The students who are against the proposition are then invited to fill the other set of chairs.

The teacher explains that there will be a debate. The students who are 'for' go first. They have two minutes in which to speak. At the end of those two minutes, the students who are 'against' have the chance to speak for two minutes. There is then a ninety-second free-for-all in which both sets of students can speak (and so debate back and forth).

After the first run through, the teacher asks the students who are against the proposition to stand up and swap places. The activity is then repeated with the new pairings. Finally, the students who are in favour of the proposition are asked to stand up and to find a partner with whom they have not yet debated. The activity is repeated for this, the third and last time.

Example

Topic: Human geography

The teacher presents the following proposition: 'More negative than positive effects result from migration.' The class is divided in two. One half is asked to argue in favour of the statement and one half is asked to argue against it. Students are divided into sub-groups, as outlined above, and given fifteen minutes to prepare their arguments. Speed Debating then ensues.

There are three important points to note about this activity. First, it is advisable for the teacher to walk around the room during the preparation period and to help students who are struggling to develop arguments. This will ensure the later debates are of a high standard and that they are sustained across the five and a half minutes which is allotted, in total, for each one.

Second, the teacher should ensure that the proposition which is presented is sufficiently debatable to afford a variety of interpretations and, in turn, a range of arguments both for and against it. A proposition which is weighted heavily in favour of one side or the other will lead to debates which are less than satisfactory.

Third, asking students to repeat the activity three times (to 'speed debate') ensures they enhance and refine the arguments they have developed (as well as the presentation of those arguments). It is probable that by the third performance pupils will have streamlined their thinking; that they will be more alive to the arguments their opponent is likely to employ; and that they will be delivering their own points with greater rhetorical skill.

Extensions and Developments

1. Instead of dividing pupils along the lines of 'for' and 'against', ask each half of the class to take on the role of an individual or group who is connected to the proposition. In the example given above this might translate as the Government Minister for Immigration and an individual from a developing country looking for a higher standard of living.

This activity works well as a precursor to an essay. Once the debates have finished, ask students to get into pairs by joining up with a member of the opposing team. The teacher turns the proposition into an essay title by adding the phrase 'To what extent do you agree?' Pairs share the arguments they earlier developed and discuss possible essay plans. Each student then produces their own piece of work, taking whatever line they choose.

13. Defend Your...

Explanation

Defending something orally or in writing requires a high level of skill. The individual needs to be able to advance their own arguments persuasively and to critique the counter-arguments which others might put forward.

In this activity the teacher can ask students to defend a variety of different things. For example:

- Defend your consequence
- Defend your cause
- Defend your reason
- Defend your argument
- Defend your claim
- Defend your interpretation
- Defend your suggestion

In each case, two things are implied: First, that whatever it is that you think or have been given is only one among many and that, as a result, you must defend it in order to show why it deserves to be taken into consideration and, in fact, why it is better, more likely or more reasonable than the other options. Second, that whatever it is you think or have been given is likely to come under attack from those who think or have been given something different. Defence must thus be both protective (why I am right) and offensive (why other possibilities are wrong).

The set-up of the activity will be determined by numbers. The following is a rough guide:

Up to 8 students = 1 circle

9 to 16 students = 2 circles

17 to 24 students = 3 circles

25+ students = 4+ circles

Students rearrange the room so that there are one or more circles of chairs. The teacher introduces the topic and explains why it is to be studied (ideally, it will be something students have already spent time learning about). Prior to the lesson, the teacher will have decided what it is they want students to defend. They will have written a series of different options on slips of paper. These are handed out to the groups of students sat in circles. Each pupil takes one slip.

Students are given a few minutes to think about the item they have been given to defend. In this time they must form an appropriate defence. They then take it in turns to reveal what their item is and to defend it to the group. Each student has one minute to mount their defence. They then have to take three questions from their colleagues and answer these in such a way as to further defend the item they have been given.

When each student has taken their turn, the group discusses the topic as a whole. Pupils continue to defend their item until the teacher feels the activity has been exhausted.

Example

Topic: Achieving sporting success

The teacher introduces the topic and explains that students will be focussing on the question: What is the main cause of sporting success? As such, each will be defending a cause. The class contains eighteen students. They form themselves into three circles. The teacher hands out the following slips, one to each student in each group:

- Innate talent is the main cause of sporting success
- Practice is the main cause of sporting success
- Coaches are the main cause of sporting success
- Luck is the main cause of sporting success
- A winning mentality is the main cause of sporting success
- Learning from your mistakes is the main cause of sporting success

Students take it in turns to announce their cause to the group and then to defend it. The questions they are asked by their peers will most likely take one of two forms:

- Questions which focus on the perceived weaknesses of the speaker's cause
- Questions which highlight the perceived strengths of other causes

In this example, where there are three separate groups, the teacher might end the activity by asking one person from each to report back to the whole class about what was said in their particular circle. A reflective discussion could then ensue in which students think and talk about the difficulties of defending a certain position and the influence (in this case) that different causes have on the point at issue (sporting success).

Extensions and Developments

1. At the end of the activity, ask students to swap slips and then to go again, this time defending something different.
2. Hand out the slips at the end of a lesson and ask pupils to prepare their defences and to anticipate possible questions for homework. As long as students complete the work, this will lead to a high level of discussion with developed reasoning and (hopefully) good use of evidence and examples.

14. Work Discussion

Explanation

The teacher sets students a major piece of work. Examples of what this might entail include an extended piece of writing, an independent project or an end-of-unit assessment. Upon finishing this, students are put into groups of three or four. A two-step process follows.

Step one: Pupils reflect in their groups on the work they have done. The teacher projects or writes onto the board a range of questions which students may choose to talk about. These could include the following:

- What did you find difficult/easy about the work and why?
- How might you improve your work next time? Why would this be an improvement? Why were you not able to do it this time?
- What did the work reveal to you about your knowledge and understanding of the topic?
- How would you have altered the task and why?
- What advice might you give to a future student who was asked to complete the task and why?

Step two: students swap their work and read through what the other people in their group have done. A discussion ensues in which each piece of work is talked about in turn. The conversation should cover what people thought of the work as well as the thinking which went into its creation. In essence, this is a peer-assessment conducted with multiple members and in dialogue. It is important to emphasise to students that the onus should be on positive comments and that suggestions for improvement should be constructive and heavily outweighed by identifications of good things about the work in question.

Example

Topic: The art of Picasso

Students are set the following piece of work: Create three sketches which make use of a range of stylistic elements employed by Picasso. Supplement this with a piece of writing outlining what elements you have chosen, why you have chosen them and how you have incorporated them in your own work.

Upon finishing (several lessons later!), students are put into groups and asked to discuss the experience of creating their own responses to the task. The teacher provides general questions as an aid to discussion, such as those noted above, as well as questions which are specific to the task. In our example, these might include:

- How did you go about choosing which stylistic elements to use?
- How did you feel about having to employ aspects of Picasso's work in your own art?
- Has the experience altered your opinion of Picasso's work? Why?

Following this, students examine, read and analyse the work of the other members of their group. A second discussion then takes place in which each piece of work is talked about in turn.

Extensions and Developments

1. Students fill in a peer-assessment pro-forma for each piece of work they examine. These are structured so that the ratio of positive comments to areas for improvement is four or five to one. The various pro-forma are given to the creators of the work, who read them through. Discussion then takes place, informed by what has been written.
2. The teacher gives all students the opportunity to alter their work as a result of what has been talked about during the discussions.

15. Formal Debate

Explanation

A formal debate is a highly structured, turn-taking discussion in which participants are bound by rules designed to create a competitive, antagonistic (in the sense that the two sides are opposed to one another) format.

A formal debate can be structured in a number of different ways. The method presented here is a standard variation.

A proposition is put forward. There are two teams, one of which is to argue in favour of the proposition and one of which is to argue against the proposition. Each team is expected to field three debaters. Their roles are as follows:

- **Proposer.** This person sets out the main thrust of the team's argument. They make the case for what it is that is being argued.
- **Seconder.** This person brings in supplementary points which add to the proposer's argument. They also rebut the arguments put forward by the opposition.
- **Closer.** This person presents a summary of their team's position and rebuts that of the opposition.

Teams are given time to prepare their arguments and to identify who will take on each role. Any team members who do not have a role are expected to help develop the team's arguments and to come up with questions which they could pose to the opposition at the end of the speeches.

The room is arranged as follows:

A table is placed at the front with a single chair. This is for the person (most likely the teacher) who will be chairing the debate. One table and three chairs are placed either side of this. These positions will be occupied by the two teams. The rest of the chairs are arranged in rows facing the tables. The remainder of the class will sit here; they will be the audience.

The debate is structured as follows:

The team in favour of the proposition go first. Their proposer speaks for three minutes, followed by the opposition team's proposer. The seconder who is in favour of the proposition then speaks for two minutes. They are followed by their opposite number. The closer who is in favour of the proposition then speaks for ninety seconds with the opposing closer following straight after. Finally, the chairperson opens the debate up to the floor so that audience members can ask questions of the two teams. All three team members are allowed to answer these questions. The debate concludes either with a vote for the winners or with the chairperson deciding which team has won. Timings are indicative and can be altered by the teacher.

Example

Topic: Developmental psychology

The teacher presents the following proposition: 'Nature rather than nurture is the key factor in human development.' The class is divided in two; one half are to argue in favour and one half are to argue against the proposition.

It is important that students are made aware of the format of the debate before they begin their preparations. This will ensure that they know exactly what is expected of them and how long they will have to talk for. The teacher should spend the preparation time flitting between the two groups and using various methods to aid them in their work.

One risk with the activity is that, if the groups are large in number, some students may end up feeling there is nothing for them to do. It can be useful to set up a series of divisions for which each group must provide workers. For example:

- Speech writers
- Question writers
- Speakers
- Identifiers of counter-arguments
- Rebuttal writers

In the debate itself, the teacher ought to take on the role of chairperson. On occasion this may be done by a student, though generally the teacher is in a better position from which to play the part. The role is that of a neutral judge who is overseeing proceedings; the job involves maintaining order, ensuring fairness and making certain both teams keep to the rules. As has been noted, the chairperson may also be required to choose a winner. If this is the case, it should be made clear well in advance what criteria will be used to make such a judgement. This will forestall any criticism of whatever decision is made.

Extensions and Developments

1. Provide the audience with peer-assessment pro-formas. These should include a range of categories such as: strength of arguments, quality of speech and use of language. Ask each student to choose two of the speakers from the opposing side

and to assess their performance. Emphasise that constructive criticism should be outweighed by positive comments.

2. Ask students to orate rather than just speak. Introduce three rhetorical devices at the start of the lesson and challenge each speaker to use at least one of them.

16. Problem-Solving

Explanation

This activity asks students to work together in order to solve one or more problems. They are expected to discuss whatever is at issue, exploring solutions as a group before arriving at some kind of consensus. It works as follows:

The teacher introduces the topic and explains why it is to be studied. The class is divided into groups of four or five. At this point, the teacher has three possible options:

- Present each group with the same problem.
- Present each group with the same set of problems.
- Present each group with a different problem.

The first option means that groups will be able to compare and contrast any solutions they come up with, either through a whole-class discussion or through a version of Envoys. This will enable them to think about the different ways in which the problem can be solved.

The second option means students will have their thinking drawn in various directions, helping them to view the topic more broadly and to make connections between different parts of it. The likelihood is that groups will work at varying speeds. This will lead to some fragmentation of the task and to students having a range of experiences.

The third option constitutes a division of labour. Each group will be dealing with a separate aspect of the topic. The results can be shared through a whole-class discussion or through a version of Envoys. Students will come to know one aspect of the topic in depth and a number of aspects at a surface level.

Whichever method is chosen, the teacher will present groups with one or more problems to discuss. It may be necessary to provide additional information so that students can get some understanding of how the problem has developed, where it came from and why it needs solving. The material can be in the form of a hand-out or a resource pack. No extra information will be required if students are already familiar with the topic or if the problem is self-explanatory.

The teacher will set a time-limit, explaining that a solution for the problem has to be developed in that period. They may also provide success criteria against which the solution will be judged. At the end of the time-limit, solutions are shared using the methods noted above, or through individual group presentations followed by questions and comments.

Example

Topic: Forces

Let us imagine that, in this case, students have already spent a number of lessons studying forces. The problems the teacher sets will thus not need to be accompanied by any additional materials. The teacher might choose to set one problem for all the groups to try and solve:

- A car manufacturer is having difficulty working out which tyres to use on their newest model. They ask you to design an experiment which would allow them to rate different tyres against each other. They would also like a set of criteria they could use to decide which tyres they should go with.

Or, they might choose to set a series of problems. Groups could work their way through these one-by-one, or they could be distributed one per group:

- How might you conduct an experiment to find out the strength of gravity on a planet other than the Earth?
- Design a product which would prevent the force of a car crash being transferred to any passengers inside the vehicle.
- Why are nuts hard to crack?
- How could you find out which type of saw was best suited to cutting through a specific type of wood?
- Design a testing range which could be used to work out the amount of force required to move a lorry at a range of different speeds and with a range of different loads.

In each of the problems listed, care has been taken to ensure there are various points which students can discuss. Constructing problems in this way means that groups will be able to maintain a debate for the duration of the activity. There will be enough for them to talk about!

Extensions and Developments

1. Have a 'super-problem' ready in case a group finishes solving their first problem inside the time which has been designated for the activity. This could be an extension of the original problem or something altogether different. Present it to students as a reward and a challenge.
2. Half-way through the activity, ask one student from each group to stand up and walk around the room. They are to listen in to the discussions other groups are having. They should take the ideas they get from this back to their original groups; fresh thinking may lead to significant changes or breakthroughs.

17. Showcase

Explanation

This activity recreates an art gallery or museum set-up in the classroom.

The teacher asks students to complete an extended piece of work. Examples include:

- A design task
- The creation of a report
- The creation of a poster presentation
- The writing of an essay
- A problem-solving activity in which the solution is explained through writing or images

The work can be done individually or in groups.

Once the task has been completed, the teacher requests that everything is cleared from pupil's desks and that the work they have created is placed in the centre of the empty space. Students are then asked to get into pairs. Each pair is given a pro-forma containing the following questions:

- What do you like about the work?

- How does the work go about answering the question/ completing the task?
- What three key strengths do you feel this work possesses?
- What one way do you believe this piece of work could be improved?

Underneath each question there is space in which students can write their answers. The question-set is repeated three times.

The teacher asks pairs to walk around the room and to look at all the different pieces of work which are on display. Pupils are invited to discuss what they see with their partner. Having viewed the entire showcase, each pair must identify three pieces of work which they want to analyse further. They return to each of these in turn and discuss them in more detail, focussing on the questions on their pro-forma (which they subsequently fill in).

When sufficient time has passed, the teacher asks students to return to their seats. A whole-class discussion ensues in which different pairs are invited to share their thoughts about the work they have discussed.

Example

Topic: Human digestion

The teacher sets the following task: In groups of three or four, produce a newspaper front cover on a sheet of A3 paper with the following headline: Scientists Discover Secrets of Human Digestive System!

Such an activity will take students quite a while. Upon finishing, they set their work out on their empty desks, form up in pairs and view what their peers have created, discussing and making notes as outlined above.

The beauty of this task is that, because students will have spent a good amount of time creating their own work, they will already have thought carefully about how the question might be answered or how the task might be completed. This means that they will be able to look at the work produced by the rest of the class with a keenly analytical eye. The discussions which result are thus likely to be of a high standard.

Extensions and Developments

1. When students have completed the task, ask them to write a reflection on their own work. This should include contrasts and comparisons with the other work they have seen.
2. At the end of the task, ask students to find the author of one of the pieces of work they have peer-assessed. They should talk to the author about their work and compare the peer-assessment with the author's own thoughts.

18. Dispute Resolution

Explanation

This activity mirrors those situations which can develop in life, whereby two parties find themselves in conflict over some matter. The discussion centres on the resolution of whatever is in dispute; students will explore the issue and the differing interpretations, arguments and perspectives which have led to the disagreement. Two alternative approaches are possible:

1. The teacher divides the class into groups of three or four. The whole class is introduced to a dispute related to the topic. Groups are asked to discuss the dispute, to produce a range of possible solutions and to decide on one of these to put forward to the rest of the class.

    The solutions proposed by each group are discussed in turn. First, it is explained why such a solution was settled on and why the group think that it will work. Second, the rest of the class question the group and the idea they have put forward. Students may also offer support if they believe the solution is a good one. Once each group's proposal has been heard and discussed, a vote is taken as to which resolution pupils think is best.

2. The teacher divides the class into groups of three or five. One student from each group takes on the role of mediator while the remaining students take on the role of opposing parties (in a group of three this means 1 vs. 1; in a group of five it means 2 vs. 2). The teacher explains what it is that is in dispute and who the opposing parties are. If possible, there will be some pre-prepared material for each group member. For the mediator this will explain their role and offer some tips on how to mediate.

For the opposing parties it will explain what their position is in the dispute and what has led them to think in it that way.

A discussion then takes place in which the opposing parties state their cases and explain why the dispute should be settled in their favour. It is the mediator's job to try and help the parties find a mutually satisfactory solution through discussion. They should prompt, ask questions, suggest alternatives and clarify the standpoints held by each student. The teacher ought to make it clear that a resolution is possible; the pupils playing the opposing parties should react in character and not be deliberately belligerent!

Example

Topic: Government industrial policy

In this example, let us imagine that students have been studying the topic for a number of lessons. Dispute Resolution is being used by the teacher to draw together various strands which have been a part of the work thus far. The following two examples refer to the two options outlined above:

1. Students are divided into groups of four and the teacher presents the class with the following dispute: 'The government wants to remove funding from a deprived area of the UK. They say that the money is not attracting investment and that the economy would be better served if funds were spent elsewhere. They have a project earmarked in an affluent area which is guaranteed to create new jobs. The people living in the deprived area are angry and claim that the government should be investing more in their region in order to attract new industries. They say that the affluent area does not need government funds and that jobs will be created there anyway.' The teacher gives groups ten minutes to discuss the dispute, to generate possible solutions and to settle on one which they will be happy putting forward to the whole class. Each group's solution is heard in turn. Further discussion and a vote take place as outlined above.

2. Students are divided into groups of five. The same scenario as above is outlined by the teacher. One person in each group takes on the role of mediator, two students take on the role of

government representatives and two take on the role of local citizens. Discussion ensues, supplemented by support materials if these are available.

Extensions and Developments

1. Give students a set of criteria which must be met for the resolution to be deemed successful. These might include things such as: both parties feel they have got something positive from the settlement; different interests are taken into account; the final resolution is predicated on clear, logical reasoning.
2. Ask the students who have played the role of mediator to talk to the class about their experiences. They should explain what it was like to be in the middle of the dispute and how they, as neutral observers, saw the arguments put forward by each of the opposing parties.

19. Planning Meeting

Explanation

This activity gives students the opportunity to discuss the various ways in which a piece of work might be approached, prior to them getting underway with the task.

The teacher sets students an extended piece of work to complete, based on what they have been studying over a series of lessons. Students are divided into groups of four. Each group is given a sheet of sugar paper and some felt-tip pens. They are invited to begin by creating a spider diagram detailing as many different approaches to the work as possible. Having done this, the group members identify which of the approaches they feel are likely to be the most successful and debate the strengths and weaknesses of each of these in turn.

At this point, students are asked to work individually to plan out the approach they will personally take. They are given between five and ten minutes. Once this has been done, they return to their groups and take it in turns to explain to their colleagues how they foresee themselves completing the task. Each approach is discussed; strengths are identified and suggestions made as to possible improvements. Finally, students go off and complete their work, using their modified plans as a guide.

It is expected that, by working through the planning stage in great detail and by being exposed to a range of viewpoints and ideas, the work which students produce will be both analytically refined and of a generally high standard.

Example

Topic: The aftermath of World War I

The teacher sets students the following task: Create a report explaining how people in France, Germany and Britain were affected by the decisions made at the end of World War I. Students are divided into groups and invited to discuss ways in which one might approach the task.

In the first stages, the emphasis is on generating ideas. In this case, a group's spider diagram could include items such as the following:

- Focus on each country in turn.
- Look at each major decision in turn and trace how it affected people in each country.
- Take certain groups common to each country (the working-class and politicians, for example) and trace how the decisions affected them.
- Compare the different effects certain decisions had on people living in each of the three countries.
- Look at the short-term, medium-term and long-term consequences of the decisions.

Many more suggestions could be added. The purpose is simply to demonstrate how one task can invite a number of different approaches, all of which are worth investigating and all of which may allow students to produce excellent work.

Identifying the strongest ideas and then using discussion to analyse these will help students to think carefully about what each might entail. The act of discussion is itself a means of planning. It will give students the chance to pick apart the various ideas and to consider how each could be effectively put into practice.

Extensions and Developments

1. When students have completed their work, ask them to re-form the original groups they were in and to share what they have

done with their colleagues. A discussion should then ensue in which the final pieces of work are compared to the plans which students outlined earlier.

2. Evaluation tables can be used as an aid to analysis. These are written tables with two columns: one for strengths and one for weaknesses. Groups can create one of these for each of the approaches they identify as being particularly strong. Individuals can then use these to help in deciding which approach to follow through with.

20. Research Discussion

Explanation

This activity involves students using discussion as a research tool. By talking to other members of the class and eliciting their thoughts, students are creating data which they can record, summarise and analyse. It works as follows:

The teacher introduces the topic and explains why it is to be studied. They then indicate that students will be researching the views and opinions of their peers. It should be clear that this means the topic ought to fall into one of two categories:

1. Something students have studied for a number of lessons and which, as a result, they already know a lot about

2. Something students already know about, or have opinions about, despite not having studied it (for example, a moral issue)

Students are asked to write five questions which they could ask their colleagues to find out what they think about the topic, or about certain aspects of it. These questions should be open so as to encourage in-depth responses. It should also be made clear that students are to engage their interviewees in discussion. This is so that further ideas and opinions can be elicited and so that elaboration is encouraged.

Next, the teacher asks all students to stand up and to find between five and ten colleagues to interview (the exact number will vary according to how much time is available). Notes should be taken during the interviews, with students recording the key points each person makes.

When the interviews have been completed, students return to their seats and write a short report summarising and analysing their results. Some of these are then read out to the whole class and form the starting point of a general discussion.

Example

Topic: Government spending

The teacher introduces the topic and asks students to develop their five questions. These might include examples such as the following:

- How do you think public money should be spent?
- How would you prioritise different public services?
- What do you feel is the right level of taxation and why?
- What is your opinion of current government spending plans?
- What do you think about proposals to measure the effects of government spending?

Here, each question is deliberately kept open. This provides plenty of scope for interviewees to talk and for interviewers to ask follow-up questions or to make comments of their own in order to generate further discussion.

Having interviewed a suitable number of their peers, students will be in a position to write up their results. It may be necessary for the teacher to provide some direct guidance here. Otherwise, there is the possibility that students might flounder and struggle to get going. A set of questions could be provided such as the following:

- Can you see any trends or patterns in your results? How might you explain these?
- Are any of your results particularly surprising? Why?
- How were people's responses similar and how were they different?

An alternative form of guidance is as follows:

1. Write a three-sentence summary for each of your questions.
2. Identify what you believe to be the most interesting thing about your results and explain why you think it is interesting.
3. Compare two or more of your summaries. What similarities and differences are there?

Having written up their results, students will be in a position to share their research findings. A whole-class discussion can develop from this point, based on what has been discovered.

Extensions and Developments

1. Challenge students to evaluate the manner in which they conducted their research and the questions which they used.
2. When students have written up their research findings, ask them to share and discuss these with three other members of the class.

CHAPTER FIVE

Conclusion

This book has been written with the teacher in mind. Twenty strategies and techniques and forty activities have been outlined, all of which are ready-to-use by any practitioner, no matter their subject. Extensions and developments have been provided for all the activities. These help teachers to differentiate and also offer suggestions as to where one might go after first starting out.

It is assumed that what has been provided is a point of departure. Users of the book will develop the contents in a way which suits them and which reflects the needs of their students. It is hoped that the activities, strategies and techniques stimulate further thinking and that they lead teachers to develop methods and approaches of their own, couched in the principles common to all high-quality discussion. It will serve us well to consider these briefly as a means by which to draw the book to a close.

Discussion should be purposeful. The teacher should have a purpose in mind, something which underpins the talk they are instigating in their classroom. Anything done without clear purpose runs the risk of falling flat or not providing students with sufficient opportunity to learn and to make progress. The teacher does not always need to share the purposes of discussion with students, though often it is helpful to do so, but they must know themselves what it is they are using discussion to achieve.

Discussion should, generally, be exploratory. There are times when disputational talk and cumulative talk (as outlined in the introduction) are the best options. In general, however, it is exploratory talk that will enable students to make the most progress. If ever one is unsure whether or not this is being achieved, return to the two key questions: Is it constructive? Is it critical? If you cannot answer yes to both of these, then consider what needs to be changed so that you can. Use the book to help.

Discussion should provide students with the opportunity to talk and to listen. Well, obviously! Yet, in the midst of a heavy workload and the feeling that one absolutely must get through the necessary content, a premise even as blatant as this can come to be forgotten. Use a variety of discussion activities, strategies and techniques in order to widen the experiences to which your students are exposed. Assess through observation, listening and reflection whether or not all students are able to talk and to listen across a series of lessons. If this is not the case, change things; try out a new activity or alter the lesson structure you usually use. Variety, so they say, is the spice of life.

And that is it. Three key principles are all one really needs: purpose, exploration and opportunity. If I had to come up with a slogan for high-quality classroom discussion, that would do nicely. The final thing to say is that I hope you have found the book useful and that it has helped you (and continues to help you) to make these principles a reality in your classroom.

Bibliography

Annas, J., *Plato: A Very Short Introduction*. Oxford: Oxford University Press, 2003.

Black, Paul, Chris Harrison, Clara Lee, Bethan Marshall, and Dylan William. *Assessment for Learning: Putting It into Practice*. Maidenhead: Open University Press, 2003.

Bruner, J. *Acts of Meaning*. Cambridge, Massachusetts: Harvard University Press, 1990.

Bruner, J. *Child's Talk: Learning to use Language*. New York: WW Norton & Co. 1983.

Bruner, J. *The Culture of Education*. Cambridge, Massachusetts: Harvard University Press, 1996.

Dewey, J. *Experience and Education*. Reprint ed. New York: Touchstone, 1997 [1938].

Donaldson, M. *Children's Minds*. London: Fontana, 1978.

Ginnis, Paul. *The Teacher's Toolkit*. Carmarthen: Crown House Publishing, 2002.

Mercer, N. *The Guided Construction of Knowledge: Talk amongst Teachers and Learners*. Clevedon: Multilingual Matters, 1995.

Mercer, N. *Words and Minds: How We Use Language to Think Together*. London: Routledge, 2000.

Plato. *Five Dialogues: Euthyphro, Apology, Crito, Meno, Phaedo*. 2nd ed. Translated by G.M.A. Grube and revised by John M. Cooper. Indianapolis: Hackett Publishing, 2002.

Taylor, C.C.W. *Socrates: A Very Short Introduction*. Oxford: Oxford University Press, 2000.

Vygotsky, L. *Mind and Society.* Edited by M. Cole, V. John-Steiner, S. Scribner, and E. Souberman. Cambridge, Massachusetts: Harvard University Press, 1978.

Vygotsky, L. *Thought and Language.* Revised and edited by Alex Kozulin. Cambridge, Massachusetts: Massachusetts Institute of Technology, 1986.

Winnicott, D.W. *Playing and Reality.* Abingdon: Routledge Classics, 2005.